Brain Dea[illegible]s and Cooking Your Way Back to Sanity

A MEMOIR

By Laura Roodman-Edwards-Roodman-Edwards-Roodman-Ray

(Not a Typo)

ISBN: 978-1-891442-59-9 • $19.95

Editor: Fran Levy
Cover Design: Diann Cage Design Co.
Cover Illustration: Drew Dinges
Layout: Amy Rosen
Proofreader, layout: Ashley Mitchell

Bluebird Publishing Co.
A division of Virginia Publishing Company
PO Box 4538
St. Louis, MO 63108
www.bluebirdbookpub.com

Acknowledgments

This book has been a joint effort from start to finish. If it were not for my entire family, this book would never have been published.

To my Mother- thank you for all of your love and support and such a wonderful birthday present.

To my sister Barb – thank you for always sticking by me, helping me however and whenever I needed it and for being the inspiration to many of my stories.

A special thank you to my brother David for all of the fantastic photography and input, and to his wife and kids – for putting up with many nights of late dinners and messy kitchens.

A very special thank you to my unbelievable sister Wendy, who has always been my partner in crime, my biggest cheerleader, and who began this project with me years ago. Thank you for the countless hours of editing, ideas (adding the recipes were her idea), and all of the work she did to get this project off the ground. There is no way I could have ever done it without her.

To my husband Tom and my kids, thank you for your unconditional love and allowing me the time to fulfill this dream of mine. I love you all more than you can imagine.

I dedicate this book to my Father who unfortunately missed most of this, but who I think would have gotten a huge kick out of it.

BRAIN DEAD IN THE BURBS

Table Of Contents

Chapter 1

The Very Quick Explanation

OK, this is my first attempt at writing — or let's just call it therapy in book form, shall we? I was sitting in my bed not being able to sleep, thinking that I've always wanted to do this and it's a hell of a lot cheaper than a $20 co-pay. Let me first very quickly introduce myself. I'm a forty-something working mom who was raised in the midwest and who married the same man with the same problems twice. (I will save that little snippet for another chapter). I was lucky enough to have had my two very pretty, high-strung, high-maintenance but wonderful daughters (who I will write about in many chapters to follow). I then was blessed to have finally met and married the strange, but very talented, sweet and brilliant love of my life. I'll just call him Sven. We've been married almost five years, and life seems exactly like it was always supposed to be: bizarre as hell, but finally in a sweet, loving, and never ever boring way.

Work-wise, I've always been in outside sales (since I failed miserably at owning my first business at age 21). Once again, you will be able to find out about that in stories to follow— I know you can't wait!

Commission sales is not an easy way to make a living, but it allowed me to pick up my kids when they did the Exorcist-like vomiting across the school parking lot without having to beg a boss for mercy. It also allowed me to pay for crazy things like food, shelter, and $42 baby shoes (isn't that just part of a master marketing plan of all shoe manufacturers, making mothers so paranoid they think that if they don't spend a stupidly large amount every 3 months, their kid will turn out with pigeon toes).

My ex-from-Hell never paid a dime (in fact I handed him a $32,000 check after I sold half of my 401K; just to get him out of my life. Do you think I just may have read the wrong book on d-i-v-o-r-c-e?)

You will learn about all these "happy pappy" things to come; but, at least now you know the basics. I will now attempt to write my first chapter to explain how this all began. In between, because you will now be one of my new best friends and know most, if not all my most deep and intimate secrets. I'm also going to give you some of my favorite recipes. I believe that each recipe fits the chapter.

See, you'll get two books in one! It will be my gift to you for reliving my strange, but never boring life! What a deal! I hope you enjoy both.

You can make this recipe and eat it while you read. Just the little bit of alcohol mixed with the cheese will help the stories seem a bit funnier.

DRUNKEN BRIE

In a small pot on medium heat combine the following:
½ Cup of Kahlua
1 Cup of brown sugar
1 cup of chopped pecans

Stir together until warm, and brown sugar has melted
Pour over a slice of brie cheese about the size of a slice of pizza
Serve with gourmet crackers and drown your sorrows or frustrations with
warm, gooey, slightly inebriated cheese.
Enjoy.

Chapter 2

CAN YOU SPELL E-N-A-B-L-E-R?

Yesterday, I found myself battling with a hormonal 13-year-old, trying to get her to the bus stop by a disgusting 6:42 AM.

I had to endure her screaming, the fact that she hadn't done her homework, telling me she was too sick and tired to go to school, deciding that she was going to be a seventh-grade dropout — all at the same time — along with the fact that she had woken up the entire household (along with a few neighbors who live close by) and made our cute, chubby little Chihuahua hide under the coffee table for fear of her life in a house that looked like a cyclone had hit it. You know, It was *that* kind of morning.

To add insult to injury, it was also pouring down raining. I barely got Maggie (the hormonal one) to get dressed by compromising with a dirty t-shirt under a pretty cute sweatshirt with a faux fur collar (that way, no one would possibly suspect that she was a total, dirty mess underneath).

She was swearing and screaming, just being her charming self, when I, the neurotic Jewish Mother-of-the-Year, totally obsessed with feeding her kids "enough," put a delicious, well-balanced, vitamin-enriched (not!) chocolate chip Eggo in the toaster. I poured her a glass of milk in her cute little blue "Maggie" plastic cup, and all the while I was counting the minutes until I wouldn't have to see her face again until the afternoon. Isn't it amazing how moms can multitask like that? I then walked down the street with this "alien child" to the bus stop.

Needless to say, my husband, who is an urban kind of very cool guy who refuses to tell people that he succumbed to living in "the burbs," still sees people peaking out the window thinking that he's in some kind of "witness protection program." He thought that I had totally lost my mind for walking a 13-year-old to the bus stop (only about 4 houses down the street). I'm sure that he thinks that my compulsive obsessiveness is a big part of the problem. The nerve!

But, as we walked down the street in the pouring rain, the Eggo waffle getting drenched and the milk spilling all over me, she continued to cry about how she's going to quit school, how she hates me, her Dad, her sister—let's just face it, everyone she knows except maybe the Chihuahua. I didn't say one word.

Finally, what seemed to be about 1-1/2 hours (but which in reality was about 3 minutes, we always cut the bus arrival pretty close, kind of like a daring suburban "Russian roulette" thing), the bus finally came. And as I watched my drenched, hormonal ragamuffin get on the bus, I don't know what came over me, but I just burst into tears.

Probably, it was the realization of what a pathetic person I was, holding a soggy Eggo and glass of milk in the pouring rain, with of course no umbrella or raincoat. All of a sudden, another neurotic (but wonderful and very sweet) mom drove up and said, "Oh Laura, you look horrible; please let me drive you back to your house!" (God forbid I should take a car in the pouring rain. No, not me; I'd rather walk in my pajamas, sweatshirt, and boots down the street so that everyone could actually see to what degree I've totally lost my mind!) I told this kind woman that she didn't have to do it; but she was so sweet, she insisted.

"Okay, thank you very much", I said, succumbing to her kindness as I was sobbing. As she drove me up the street, she told me that she was having the same "hormonal hell" in her family and that this too will pass. (When, how, and will I be alive to see it happen?) I told her to drop me off, and she said, "No, you look so horrible; let me drive you to the back of your house so that you won't have to walk"

Just as I told her that she didn't have to and that I had never seen anyone drive so fast in reverse, the car slammed into the side of our home. Neither of us was hurt, but, I felt horrible that I was the reason she now had a huge dent in her car.

Later that day, when I had told another one of my friends what had happened, I was crying, but she had the audacity to laugh at my story (the nerve!). I said, "What the hell is so funny, Linda?" and she said, "Laura, I've always thought that you could write a newspaper column or a book about your life. Your life is just so strange, no one will ever believe it!"

Well, I do think that she meant this to be a compliment (in a strange and twisted way; but what the hell, a compliment is a compliment, right?) Anyway, that is why I started this. And who knows? Maybe, just maybe, I'll be able to quit my day job (or then again, maybe not!).

Some people like to mask their frustrations by having a nice cocktail. I, on the other hand, like to soften my sorrows with about a half a pan of these "edible orgasmic" blueberry bars. If I'm really depressed, I top it off with some vanilla bean ice cream. These are always a hit and will make your house smell wonderful.

UNBELIEVABLY DELICIOUS BLUEBERRY BARS

Preheat oven to 350 degrees
2-1/2 Cups of flour
1 Cup (2 sticks) of melted salted real butter
1 Cup sugar
1 Cup chopped pecans
Mix up until crumbly
1-16 oz jar of blueberry or raspberry preserves (you could use lemon, strawberry, or blackberry, too.)
In a 9 x 13 inch buttered and floured pan, pat down ¾ of mixture in the pan.
Spread preserves to 1/8 inch from the edge of the pan (if you go too close to the pan, the preserves will burn)
Crumble the rest of the flour mixture on top of the preserves.
Bake for 45 minutes or until golden brown.
Once it's out of the oven and cooled for about 10 minutes, cut into squares before it totally cools.

Chapter 3

"And The Academy Award Goes To The Bleached Blonde With Black Roots And Green Feet"

Let me preface this chapter by explaining that I met my ex when I was young, naïve and stupid. You may wonder as you read ahead whether anyone could be as gullible as I was. You'll think this is all B.S. Unfortunately, to my humiliation, it's the truth, the whole truth…and nothing but, blah, blah, blah.

I also want to tell you that, growing up in the burbs of a midwestern city – in a neighborhood 47.5 percent Catholic and a 42 percent Jewish - we were considered the "poor Jews" and just a little odd. I never quite fit in. Never had a date in high school. Okay, I lied. Sorry. I did date the dishwasher at the local restaurant where I waited tables – once. The date was totally ruined when he scared the crap out of me and asked me if I "bonged?" I looked at him and didn't know what he was talking about, and said "I'm not sure, but definitely not on the first date!"

The ex was 10 years older than me, co-owned several small pizzerias in small towns with populations of 30,000 or less, and was quite a handsome guy, totally out-of-the-ordinary from the type of guys that I was used to. I couldn't believe he actually wanted to ask me out on a date. Me, a socially awkward "almost virgin" (that's for a later chapter), who weighed in at a whopping 168 pounds (and that was 38 pounds less than when I'd started my diet).

At the time, I was working at my first real sales job, had just bought my first (very small and very green) house, drove a cute white Chrysler convertible (always with the top down — and the heat on if it was freezing outside), and for the most part, thought

I was pretty darn hot.

One of the requirements of my sales job was that our "crew" (a group of about five salespeople, mainly made up of men who were all pretty slutty and who stayed away from me because they knew I was so totally clueless and they would never get "lucky") would have to stay in these small towns to sell Yellow Pages ads for a few weeks until the book was completed.

So, this is how I came to meet "Dick." Later on, when I realized that he had problems with alcohol, I renamed him like that Joanne Woodward movie *The Three Faces of Eve*. I lovingly named him "Dick White" (when he was sober) and "Dick Black" (when he was drunk and disgusting). Now I just call him "Psycho Dick," or "P.D." for short.

Anyway, I had to live in one of these small towns where he had a restaurant. Having just lost about 38 pounds and not having had a date in quite some time (about a half a decade, but who's counting?), I decided to break my biggest rule and go out with a customer.

He asked me if I had ever been horseback riding. I was trying to be as cool as I could and said, "Oh yes, I love riding!" (The truth is that the only time I had ever been on a horse was at a low-end amusement park where you paid 50 cents to get on a pony and an old man with a couple of teeth would walk you around a smelly arena for three minutes). He quickly said, "Great! Get your riding clothes and meet me here in an hour."

I was pretty giddy about doing this. So, I ran back to my hotel and changed into my most earthy, countrified clothes. When he looked at me in my three-and-a-half-inch high heeled boots, tight jeans (to show off, of course, my new figure — even though I had to lie down on the hotel's bed to zip up the damn things), and gray cowl-neck cashmere sweater (the first thing I ever bought at Nordstrom's), he said, "Where would you like to change into your riding clothes?" I replied, in my very confident tone of voice, "Oh no, I'm sorry, these ARE my riding clothes.

So, we then went on a two-hour *ride from Hell* with his friends, who had names like Buffalo Phil, Suck-em Up Steve, and Roundabout Randy. (I could not have made up these names!)

So, here was this clueless Jewish girl who couldn't breathe in her jeans and whose life was passing her by as we went down these shale cliffs. I guess this was the definitive test of what a good salesperson I was (translation: bullshitter), because I had everyone fooled into believing that I knew exactly what I was doing on this horseback ride "from Hell" until the very end.

Finally, we stopped. I hadn't had even one drop of water, because I thought ahead of time and knew that #1- I couldn't pee in the woods (especially without toilet paper), and #2, there was the problem of having to zip my jeans back up (by lying down on the ground and sucking in my gut, which would probably result in my getting poked with a thousand of those painful midwestern cactus and tumbleweed things).

When I finally got off the horse, as the guys were guzzling their beers, I realized my feet were swollen from those damned boots. I took them off and headed toward this cute little pond in the middle of wherever we were. I think it was called South Bumblef*&% Nowhere.

All of a sudden, I saw these beautiful little lily pads and had this "aha moment." I thought to myself, "This will be a perfect thing for my aching feet!!" I then thought, "I bet this is what 'country people' do all the time. Instead of nice pedicures and foot rubdowns from nice little Vietnamese women who laugh and talk about your goofy-looking toes in their native tongue, women just become one with Earth and use what God has provided for free. (Very deep, I know).

Anyway, as I was in my own little world squishing my aching toes in the warm lily pads, I looked up and saw the four guys looking at me in bewilderment and shock. Dick White, two beers away from being Dick Black screamed, "What the hell are you doing?" I said, "Oh, I'm just relaxing and helping my aching feet with the help of these lily pads." The guys burst out laughing, spitting up their beer, and then Dick shouted, "Those aren't lily pads, for God's sake, they're cow pies!"

Well, my cover was completely blown, and I had to live with green feet for about three weeks.

GREEN KEY LIME COW PIE

Crust:
1 ¾ Cups graham cracker crumbs
¼ Cup sugar
6 Tablespoons of real, unsalted butter, melted

Filling:
6 Yolks from extra-large eggs, at room temperature
¼ Cup sugar
1 14-oz. can sweetened condensed milk
2 Tablespoons lime zest
¾ Cup lime juice, freshly squeezed (4-5 limes)

Topping:
1 Cup heavy cream - cold
¼ Teaspoon vanilla extract
¼ Cup sugar
Lime slices and/or lime zest

Preheat oven to 350 degrees.

Combine graham cracker crumbs, sugar and butter in a bowl. Press into a 9-inch pie pan. Bake for 10 minutes, until golden brown. Make sure it is completely cooled.
Then, beat egg yolks and sugar with electric mixer at a slow speed, 5 minutes or until thick. On medium speed, add the condensed milk, lime juice and zest. Pour into the pie shell and freeze.

For the topping, beat the heavy cream with mixer on medium-high speed until soft peaks form. Add the sugar and vanilla. Spoon onto the pie and decorate with either lime slices and/or lime zest. Using both makes for a pretty cow pie. Freeze again.

You will get rave reviews from people on this one– even from those whose favorite pie is key lime. They will tell you it is the best ever!

Chapter 4

Wasn't That Old Saying, "Intellligence Is In The Eyes Of The Beholder"?

(I Know It Was "Beauty," But "Intelligence" Fits The Story So Much Better)

One Saturday afternoon, after a day of running around like an idiot trying to do the whole week's errands, I decided to give my kids a treat and take them to the neighborhood pizza place. My daughters were, I think, 8 and 10 at the time. Maggie, the oldest, had a friend with her (I'll call her "Alexandra"). Let me just mention here that Maggie (like 97.2 percent of all kids now) has been diagnosed with one of those alphabet labels: ADD, ADHD, OCD, etc. I always said "No, my kid is not ADD; she's just S.P.O.I.L.E.D. You may already have noticed that I tend to digress a little. let me just tell you this little story quickly.

Maggie has always been a little scattered. Very cute and as sweet as she can be (more of the time; especially in front of strangers), but just a little naive (10 going on 8 years old — which, although sometimes infuriating, is preferable to 10 going on 19). So this just means that at the same time that I feel like slitting my wrists, I'm counting my blessings.

Finding true friends has always been a challenge for Maggie, because she's just not "easy." Anyway, this friend, Alexandra, is basically perfect in every way (little bitch — no, not really, just in the eyes of a mother whose daughter has ADD) She is a beautiful half-Asian and half-Israeli girl. It'll make sense later in my story. Anyway, it was Maggie, Alexandra, Mollie (my youngest) and me.

We finally were able to sit down and have lunch at around 2:00 pm on this Saturday afternoon. We ordered our food. Of course, being a neurotic Jewish mother (both food obsessed and guilty about depriving these children of nourishment since 8:00 am), I ordered enough food to make it look like we were at "Old Italian Country Buffet".

As we were eating, Maggie was trying to be very nice by starting a conversation, "Mommy, did you know that Alexandra has NEVER gotten a B in her entire life? She has never gotten less than 100 percent on all of her tests, EVER!" Well, as the mature and wonderful mother that I am, I actually wanted to stick my finger down my throat and puke. But instead, I did the correct and mature "mother thing" and said "Wow, Alexandra, that is so wonderful. What a fantastic accomplishment!" (Barf.) "Your mom and dad must be so proud of you! How have you done it? Do you just study all of the time?" She looked at me and said politely, "Well actually, Mrs. Ray, it comes quite naturally to me." I said, "Really, why is that?" And she said, "Well, as you already know, my mother is a piano virtuoso and my father is a brain surgeon. And in fact, I don't know if you already know this, but, my great grandfather's second cousin was Albert Einstein."

My 8-year-old just looked at her and stared with her huge brown eyes. She paused and then screamed. "Wow, Alexandra, that is so COOL! Does that mean you get all the bagels you want for free?" *[1]

I'm thinking that this would be a good time for some "brain food."

This next recipe is my sister Gwendolyn's fabulous halibut recipe (it is so delicious that I even dream about it sometimes). I also just like to say, "How about some halibut for the hell of it?" Aren't I clever?)

(Footnotes)

1 A Midwest chain is Einstein Bros. Bagels.

MEDITERANEAN HALIBUT FOR THE HELLUVIT
à LA GWENDOLYN

Preheat oven to 425 degrees

4-5 Fish fillets, 6 to 8 oz. each
4 Roma (plum) tomatoes, seeded and dried
2 Tablespoons calamata olives
¼ Cup capers, drained
1 Teaspoon minced garlic
3 Tablespoons olive oil
3 Tablespoons fresh lemon juice
2 Teaspoons minced shallots
¼ Cup dry white wine
2 Tablespoons fresh basil
Salt and pepper to taste

Mix these 10 ingredients and let stand for 45 minutes.

Brush the filets with a little olive oil. Top fillets with the tomato mixture.

Wrap each piece of fish in parchment paper and fold carefully into a "pocketbook."

Place each piece of wrapped in an ovenproof baking dish suitable for table service.

Bake at 425 degrees for 15-20 minutes, unwrap carefully and serve.

(Please let me know what you think and if you end up dreaming about it, too!)

Chapter 5

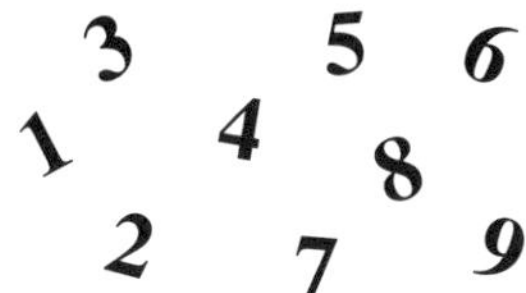

The One And Only Thing I Have In Common With Louis Farrakhan

Well, besides the fact that we breathe the same air and live on the same planet, there is only one thing I have in common with this man. Sven loves to point it out as often as the conversation allows, which really is not that often.

My husband hates it whenever I speak of the non-scientific, only for fun, horoscope-like, don't-take-it-too-seriously study of numerology. Though I don't live by it, I actually paid $25 for a reading in a double-wide trailer to learn about it. What I found from the mystical wisdom of "Swami Samantha" helped me to understand why I have made the mistakes I have throughout the years.

I should tell you that, once a year, I dress up like a goofy gypsy for a Mother/Daughter Girl Scout sleepover in the school gymnasium. (This is as uncomfortable as it gets!) They all call me "Swami Mommy." I think it is such a hoot how the line goes all the way across the gym for all the Suburbiaville moms and daughters waiting to get "readings" from ME!

During Louis Farrakhan's Million Man March a few years ago, he was spouting a lot of mean rhetoric (which he does so well), much of which was directed against Jewish people. Besides talking about how horrible 95 percent of the world is, he also spoke a lot about the enormous powers of Numerology. That killed any "open mindedness" Sven could possibly have had on this non-scientific study that I thought was so interesting. If Louis Farrakhan believes in it, it must be full of "ca-ca" ("shit" in Spanish) To say that my husband knows more about current events, history, and anything else you can think of is the understatement of the millennium.

Okay, so now let me explain the very rudimentary foundation of numerology (à la Laura Ray, through the teachings of "Swami Samantha"). Please do not quote me on any of this crap. I'm just telling my new best friends (that would be you) what it cost me 25 bucks to learn. See, not only will you get a memoir and new recipes, but a lesson of numerology all in one book. What a deal! Today is certainly your lucky day!

According to Swami Samantha, everyone has nine lives (kind of like kitty cats), and by referencing your birth date you can find out which life you are in. This "mystic formula" is very easy; you can even figure it without a calculator.

Add up the date of your birth until you get a single digit. For example, if your birthday is 1/12/1995, you would add

1 + 1 + 2 + 1 + 9 + 9 + 5, which equals 28.

Now add together the two numbers making 28:

2 + 8 = 10. Then add together the two numbers making 10:

1 + 0 = 1.

So, this person is a "1," or in Swami Samantha lingo, "In their first life."

Let's do this again. Isn't it fun?

If your birthday is 2/25/2003, you would add

2 + 2 + 5 + 2 + 0 + 0 + 3, which equals 14. Then add

1 + 4 = 5. This person is a "5" (Same as me; please read on for the sad findings.)

A synopsis of the theory is that 1's, 2's, and 3's are in their "learning years," and nothing comes easily to them. No one has given them anything or handed them anything on that proverbial "silver platter". Even though they will become very successful, 1's, 2's, and 3's always end up going two steps forward and one step back. It's always difficult for them to decide what they want to be when they grow up.

I don't know that much about 4's, but I do know that if you're a 4, you are in your "career" life, and it's difficult for you to "multi-task." Whatever you decide to do at the time, you will excel at it, but your focus is usually very narrow. Most of the time, you do what you have picked (whether it is to be the perfect housewife, physician or hockey player) to perfection and talk about it, breathe it, live it to the utmost.

If you are a 5, your entire life revolves around family, love, relationships, and (of course) sex. Nothing else really seems to matter. You are loyal to a fault. Money, your job, and so forth, are only a means to an end, which is to have great friendships, a wonderful family, and (please pardon my French), having great sex with the person you love as often as possible.

If you are a 6, you are in your "money" life. Nothing else really seems to matter. Sixes end up most of the time having a lot of money; or, if they don't, it ends up ruling their lives.

The 7's, 8's, and 9's are "wise old souls." Everything comes quite easily for them. They usually have the upper hand in relationships, especially in love relationships. They are the ones who can either stop or start any relationship. Each of these "wise old souls" has a characteristic that is unlike all the others: 7's have problems with addiction (it's either them or those around them who have addiction problems.) (Psycho Dick is a 7. Need I say more?)

Eights are generous to a fault — until you piss them off. Then 8's are characteristically cold as ice and are able to cut off relationships in a millisecond. And finally, 9's are supposedly the "wisest of wise old souls." They are (according to Swami Samantha) superior, and usually can do or be anything they want. They have control over the masses and they know it.

So now you have it — the entire Laura Ray School of Numerology.

Now, I can show you why I believe in it (in a fun way, of course. I promise I'm not going to join a strange cult any time soon. Anyway, I hate wearing those ugly orange robes — definitely NOT my color!)

As I told you in the first chapter, I was 24 when I met Psycho Dick, and even though by that time I had lived in Spain and Mexico, put myself through college, lived in several different states and was somewhat successful (for a 24-year-old), I was embarrassingly as socially awkward. My few relationships with men were horrible, and I never ever knew how to act around them. To put it bluntly, I couldn't walk, talk, or breathe around men — especially around those I found attractive.

When I met this strange, handsome, cowboy kind of guy, this

successful entrepreneur in the middle of nowhere, I was pretty dumbfounded (in a 24-year-old way.) He really was very handsome back then. Now he kind of looks like Grandpa Munster, and I have to continually show the girls pictures of what their biological Dad used to look like, because I think it scares them that they will favor him when they get older! It's a terrible thing to see what alcohol and drugs can do to someone's looks. P.D. could easily be the poster child for "Here is your Body before drugs — and here is your body after drugs." If that picture wouldn't scare the crap out of any kid thinking about taking a drink, smoking, pill popping or snorting, nothing would! (Trust me on this.)

Anyway, I guess it was about me finally feeling better about myself. I had just lost about 40 pounds (still a size 14 or 16, but much better than size 24). Or it was about him just knowing all the tricks (which I won't go into. Say "Thank you, Laura." Trust me, it's T.M.I.) But, when we finally did make love, I had my very first orgasm .(See, we ARE best friends, now. I can tell you the truth about my sex life after bonding over only five chapters.)

It was like, Well hell, after that feeling, nothing else seemed to matter at *all.*

Oh, you're ten years older than me? *That's okay.*

Oh, you have five daughters between the ages of 3 and 13 from your wayward ex-wife? *No big deal. In fact, my favorite movie of all time is the The Sound of Music, and I know that I'll love the girls and they'll love me, and who knows, if I have some spare time, I'll make their clothes out of some of your old draperies from the restaurant....*

Oh, I'm going to have to sell my cute $49,000 green house and live above a small town, smelly pizzeria with facing toilets? I can do that!

Oh, I'm going to have to move out of a big, metropolitan, thriving city to a small, backwards town where they think that Jews really do have horns? I'll change their way of thinking, I know I can!

Oh, I'm going to have to quit my wonderful job that pays me more than $60K and live in a town where the best job I could get is at the small town newspaper that was named after a political party that disappeared more than 100 years ago (the Whigs)? Maybe I'll be able to change their political views. I'm good at those kinds of things!

The list could go on and on, but I think you get the point, and I don't want you to lose any more respect for me than you have already, especially this early in the book.

All I can say is, **damn that orgasm!** (I'll bet you don't hear that very often.)

Probably the saddest thing of all, was that orgasm was not just the first but probably the last one I had with Psycho Dick. Of course, the thrill died the minute I said "I do," and Dick White turned into Dick Black, who quickly morphed into Psycho Dick. Another stupid trait of a "5" is that once they make a commitment, that's it. (For me, 14 years of *commitment hell.*)

The only reason I told you all this was to explain why my family, friends, and now, my loving, sweet, giving, respectful, hilarious, and yes, very sexy husband are so important to me. They are absolutely the only reason I exist. Yes, I know that I'm being a bit heavy, but it's really true, and now, thanks to Swami Samantha, I know it's not my fault..

So, I guess that is why, from now on, after years of therapy, I'm just going to apologize for my stupidity by just saying seven simple words:

"I can't help it — I'm a 5!"

I sometimes feel as though I've wasted a huge part of my "5" life. It should have really been a lot more fun. All I know is that right now, I'm trying to make up for lost time!

HELGA'S ORGASMIC BROWNIES

Preheat oven to 350 degrees

(4) 4 oz. Squares of semi-sweet baking chocolate
1 Cup (2 sticks) of salted butter
2 Cups of sugar
4 Eggs, room temperature
1 Cup flour
1 teaspoon vanilla
2-1/2 Cups of mini marshmallows
1 Cup semi-sweet chocolate chips
1 Cup chopped walnuts

In a large saucepan, melt butter and the 4 chocolate squares over low heat. Remove from heat and add the sugar. Blend well.

Beat in one egg at a time into the chocolate mixture. Do this by hand; don't use a beater or electric mixer. Stir in the flour and mix well. Add the marshmallows, chocolate chips, and walnuts. Mix thoroughly.

Pour into a buttered and sugared (I use sugar instead of flour – the taste is better) 9" x 13" pan.
Bake for 45 to 50 minutes until done.

Cut after 10 minutes, when they are still warm

Chapter 6

I'm Teaching A New Class Called "How To Divorce A Friend 101"

Sven had lunch with his son the other day. His son is a fantastic 23-year-old who I love to death. He's very sweet, and he really took well to having two high-maintenance, high-strung new sisters. I'm sure it wasn't an easy feat for him because he was an "only child" for the first 17 years of his life, and then all of a sudden he inherited all of us. He has really handled it well, and for that I'm so very grateful for him every day of my life. Yes, I know that I'm sounding just a wee bit dramatic, but after living through the "five stepdaughters from hell" for 14 years and counting, (and I did just get a call from a bill collector yesterday afternoon) Sven Jr. is, to say the very least, a "welcome relief."

Anyway, when Sven came home that evening he told me that he and his son had a very interesting conversation while they were eating lunch at their favorite Indian restaurant. It was a talk he had wanted to have for quite some time with his son. He told Sven Jr. that, when he fell in love, to make sure that the woman he falls in love with has many "girlfriends."

I thought that was insightful of my very smart husband. He realized that was what was lacking in all his past girlfriends — and believe me, the list is pretty damn long. I was actually the first woman he ever dated, much less married, who actually had a lot of girlfriends. This is truly a huge revelation. When you think about it, it is important and it does say a lot about women who really don't like other women or who are not able to keep friends.

These women are usually the ones who would much rather have

"guy" friends than a group of really good "girlfriends." We all know women like this. Not very well of course — they won't let us! But, I'm sure that everyone who is reading this knows at least one or two women who fit into this category.

Unfortunately, I have found in my many years on this Earth that these women are competitive with other women, in both the business world and the real world. I'm not your "stereotypical stereotyper," (I just made that term up), but these are the women who are prone to having affairs with other women's men. They are the ones who make your work life a living hell. They are the ones that look you up and down as if you needed to be on "What Not to Wear." And of course these are the women who can't stand when you're in a better place than they are. I know you get the gist of what I'm trying to say.

This brings me to my little story. I, Laura Ray, have many girlfriends. In fact, because of my severe social awkwardness when it comes to men, I never really had any guy friends except for my brother and Sven, if they even count. This may sound stupid beyond words, but it was actually tougher on me to divorce two of my best girlfriends than it was to divorce Psycho Dick, the man who I married twice and had two children with. Let me try to explain.

You may ask yourself, how strange is this Laura Ray? Well, I'll tell you. At the end of my marriage with P.D., I hated him so viscerally that I would literally fall out of our king-size bed at least twice a week because I had been sleeping "that close" to the edge to avoid smelling him, touching him, or (God forbid) arousing him (kill me, please!). I would end up falling on my ass in the middle of the night. It never was a pretty sight.

Actually, the day that I filed for divorce for the second and final time (Valentine's Day 2000 — very romantic, wouldn't you say?), was one of the happiest days of my life. On the other hand, the days that I divorced my two very close girlfriends were some of the saddest days I've experienced. I was thinking about going through some sort of divorce group therapy class for it, but I thought everyone in the group might think that I was a total *wackjob*.

I just think it goes against the grain of the "normal" woman (the one who is loyal and deeply loves her close friends as if they were their own sisters) to ditch a friend. I always thought that if I were to ever hit a huge jackpot or lottery or make a lot of money getting on the "Wheel of Fortune" or something stupid like that, I would split my windfall with all my best friends. It was that Golden Rule thing creeping up on me again.

When I finally realized that these two friendships of mine were actually toxic, I accepted (with the urging of everyone I know) that I had to cut them off immediately. At the end of the chapter, I'll give you the one recipe that helped me get through these traumatic times. It's really quite a miracle how something that has chocolate cake, caramel, Heath bars, chocolate chips, and mounds of whipped cream in it can help you get through tragic times such as these.

I'll tell you about my first "girlfriend divorce" very quickly. Tina (of course all of the names have been changed to protect the "Not Bitchy") and I were great friends. We had a group of about five friends who all worked together for more than a decade, but it was really she and I who were the closest of friends. We had lunch together about four times a week. We would work out together, decide together what our goals were every few months, and constantly be each other's biggest cheerleader. We were even very close to purchasing a franchise together. I loved her with all my heart. Not only did we have the same stresses, because we had the same commission sales job, but we went through our divorces together and were also single moms together. So, we really understood each other perfectly (so I thought). I would have done *anything* for Tina, and I really think she would have done the same for me — UNTIL I met Sven, found a better job, and was happy for the first time in about 42 years.

My mom used to say that "You can always tell who your true friends are during the bad times." I do think that is true, but I found out in this particular situation that you can also find out who your true friends are during the best times of your life and when you're the happiest you've ever been. Looking back, painful as it is, I have to say that during our 16 years of friendship, Tina never saw me truly happy. I think deep down she liked that I was struggling on the love front and the home front and had the same pressures at work that she did. When I finally found Sven and got a much better-paying job, and the girls were settling down and showing signs of healing from the destructive Psycho Dick crap (we'll call that D.P.D.C. for short), I think it upset her proverbial "apple cart." She really didn't know how to handle the fact that I was happy. In her own way, she tried to sabotage my relationship with Sven and my relationships with some of our other closest longtime friends. This hurt me so badly, I remember coming home and sobbing. Still, years later, I don't fully understand why she did some of the things that she did.

I'm over this "divorce." It took a longer time to heal from this one than it did with P.D. It seemed like such a huge betrayal to me. It also took the views of others who I respect to confirm that I wasn't losing my mind over this. Sven actually asked me to not invite her to our wedding. I was shocked. Here was a woman who probably would have been one of my Maids of Honor, besides my two sisters and the two goofy flower girls, Maggie and Mollie of course, who pelted rose petals at the roaring attendees. I didn't even invite her to the most joyous night of my life. Sven just looked at me and simply said, "Hell, Honey, why would you invite Judas, the White Bellied Rat to our wedding?" Once again, in a dozen words and in his own subdued way, my man knocked it right out of the ball park.

The only other "best friend divorce" I had wasn't nearly as painful. In fact, it was pretty damn cathartic and should have happened years ago, but as you can tell by my other chapters, divorce isn't something I do very well. "Diana" was my girlfriend mainly because my first boss, a man who I respected and greatly admired, had asked me if I would be his wife's friend. They were new to the area and she didn't really have many friends (Could that be Clue #1?). Have you ever had a friend that you always had fun with? Someone in whom you saw qualities that were good, even though no one else did? This was Diana in a nutshell. She was knockdown gorgeous, used to be a rock star's groupie (I don't think I'd better mention his name), and to understate it, she was probably the biggest *Legend in her Own Mind* of anyone I've ever met. Even when I had to keep my opinions to myself and swallow my pride, I always found her to be a hoot. Things always happened around her, and she would say and do things that I would never in my entire life think to say or do.

From now on, in this story, I'm going to call her "Friend "ID." Kind of like the Addams Family's "Cousin Itt," but with a Freudian twist. Do you remember Sigmund's theory (yes, we're on a first-name basis) of the Id, the Ego, and the Super Ego? The Id is the stage of life (usually as an infant) where you have mostly hedonistic tendencies, devoid of any conscience whatsoever. Well, that is how I felt when I spent time with her. I knew it was wrong, I knew that she did and said terribly hedonistic things all the time that always ended up making her feel wonderful and those around her feel like crap.

Other friends and relatives didn't see Friend Id as interesting or entertaining as I did. In fact, a great example of her personality occurred one Sunday morning when I had invited her over to my parents' home for a nice Sunday brunch (because her husband was out of town and she was all alone with her huge ego). As we were all eating the normal Jewish 12,000-calorie brunch fare like lox, bagels, knishes, corned beef, whitefish, noodle kugel, blintzes, fried potatoes, and so forth. Friend Id decided to tell my two sisters that she never understood why people end up being overweight. She started spouting stuff like "Why can't people realize that if they would just increase their aerobic activity and decrease their caloric intake everyone would be at their proper weight?" Well, needless to say, you couldn't have said a more stupid thing to my family. Each of us has had our own struggles with weight.

Within about one second (it might have been faster than that), my older sister Babs grabbed my arm, took me into the living room and said, *"Who the hell is this bitch? What broom did she ride in on? Please Lou, Get her the f*%& out of this house before I kill the skinny bitch!"* I got it. You know, I'm pretty smart about being able to read people. It doesn't take a broom to fall on my head to let me know that I'd better get Friend Id out of my parents' house quickly, which of course I did.

Anyway, I was able to forgive her for all her stupid comments throughout the years because in a way I felt kind of sorry for her for being so damn clueless. And yes, I was one of her only three friends. The "Id Posse" would have been reduced greatly if I were to leave the fold, and then I would have felt so badly for those I left behind.

Well, years went by and I was always able to let things go. I couldn't even talk about her to my "un-Id" friends and family. They all thought I was a total masochist for having her as a friend. They loved me, so they overlooked this huge flaw in my personality. That was, until she did something to me that was completely inexcusable.

It took me years and years to get pregnant with Maggie. My OB-Gyn told me that he didn't think it would be possible for me to get pregnant. I totally forgot that you had to have sex to get pregnant. I also had the stress of living with an abusive alcoholic, and it did strange things to my body. I stopped having periods and I couldn't touch the guy I was married to without wanting to throw up.

When I found out that I was pregnant, I was beyond elated. I went with Babs to the doctor and she immediately ran out and bought me all types of very expensive maternity clothes that I couldn't afford and a beautiful, brand new, leather rocking chair. I was in heaven. I didn't care if I was going to have to raise this child alone; I just always knew that I wanted to be a mom more than anything else.

To say that the pregnancy was stressful is an understatement. I had morning sickness every day of the pregnancy, had to work up until the day my water broke, had to deal with the fact that P.D. was not working, dealing with all of his daily verbal abuse, worrying about how the hell we would pay the water bill, as well as living with that nagging question, "What the hell am I doing bringing an innocent child into the mess I'm in right now?"

OK, now that you have the picture, I was in the hospital bed after having just given birth to my beautiful, big-headed, bald, 7 pounds, 13-ounces, healthy baby girl. My entire family had left to have dinner and drinks after the delivery. P.D. stayed with me for a loving 4 minutes after her birth and then disappeared to who knows which bar. He later told me that he ended up drivng to his home town, which was about three hours away, so that he could tell everyone that he was a father for the sixth time. I think he may have forgotten that there was that tricky little invention called the telephone? Anyway, I found myself all alone with my baby, which really was pretty lovely.

I was still bloody and sweaty, looking like death warmed over. I was holding my gorgeous baby, finally realizing that this was why God put me on this Earth. I was having a very deep moment. It may have been hallucinations from lack of food, lack of oxygen, epidural anesthesia, and insurmountable pain. Whatever it was, we need to bottle that feeling and sell it so we'll all be able to quit our day jobs.

I was having my glowing moment and in walks Diana. I swear, as God is my witness, she was wearing a full-length fur coat, long dangly diamond earrings (which I think her married Rock Star boyfriend gave to her in the 70s), and an outfit that I think she purchased just in case she was ever invited to go to the Academy Awards.

Here I am, bloody and sweaty, tears of happiness falling profusely down my face, and she says in her sweet Texan drawl, "So, how was it, darling?" I said as I was sniveling, "Oh Diana, it was absolutely perfect! It couldn't have been easier! They gave me an epidural, I 'hoo hoo heed' three or four times, and out popped this gorgeous baby!"

Without hesitation she said, "Well, of course she popped out quickly!" I looked at her, not quite sure what she meant until she went on to say, "Honey, with your size hips, of course the baby will come out without any trouble at all! Don't you know, you have those Plantation Women hips! God made women like you so that back in the frontier times, you could just squat in a field and have babies! You are sooooo lucky." She then continued with, "I, on the other hand, am not so lucky. My Doctor said that he had never seen anyone with smaller hips than mine. When I had Tiffany Nicole, they had to use pliers and all the life support paraphernalia they could find because of my small, small hips. Her poor little head was cone shaped for several weeks!" She then continued (would she EVER SHUT THE F*&% UP? The answer, of course, was NOOOOO!), "Look at Maggie's head, it's perfectly round. That is of course because of your enormous hips. You are so lucky!" She must have said the "You are so lucky" shit about seven times. Well, in those 6 minutes, she totally ruined what should have been the most magical moment of my life. Forget the fact that the father of this beautiful, healthy baby was getting shitfaced, that I was left all alone, and that I still hadn't taken a shower or gotten something to eat.

All I could think of is, "I must divorce this friend who just told me that I had Plantation Woman Hips." It was quite an easy thing to do. No second thoughts, no hesitation at all, no guilt, no anything at all except the knowledge that I had to get this woman out of my life immediately. It was just not healthy for me (or her) to have her in my life.

I will now give you, my new "best friends," one of my favorite recipes of all time. You are all women who have many girlfriends and who would never have said anything like what Ex- Id Friend said to me after I'd given birth. This is one of my signature recipes that I bring everywhere; and honestly, it's the one that I ended up making and eating at least once a week for a year after I gave birth and divorced Best Friend #2. It definitely helped me maintain my "plantation hip" status!

GRANDMA BETTY'S DELICIOUS HEATH BAR CAKE

Preheat oven 350 degrees

Bake 1 dark chocolate cake mix per instructions in a buttered and floured 9 x 13 pan.

While it is still warm, poke holes all over the cake (I usually use the handle of a wooden spoon so that the holes are fairly large)

Pour one small can of Borden's sweetened condensed milk in the holes, spreading the rest all over the cake.

Then pour one jar of caramel ice cream topping on the cake and spread that evenly over the top.

Cover and refrigerate cake for at least 4 hours (I try to do it overnight if I can).

Ice the cake with a large container of Cool Whip.

Then, generously decorate the cake with Heath Bar or Skor baking bits (found in the baking section of the grocery store) and miniature chocolate chips.

Refrigerate for an hour and serve.

Chapter 7

The Day That My Life Span Was Shortened By Ten Years

Maggie, as I've said before, is high strung, anxious, naïve, goofy, and pretty damn cute (spoken by a very biased mom). I always said, "The reason why God gave me children so late in life is that by the time my kids are 16 years old, I'll be dead!" This little story will explain why I say that..

At the public school that the girls go to, they have an age-appropriate "Life Skills" class in the fourth and fifth grades explaining the basic facts of life. Well, I had been asking Maggie every day after school if she wanted to talk about anything, if she had any questions about anything, and so forth, hoping and praying that she would say "No." She did probably have questions for me, but I just thought she was just too embarrassed to ask; and being the weasel mother that I am, I just took the "No thanks" as a "Thank God!"

A few months passed. It was an absolutely gorgeous Saturday afternoon. Why oh why, do these little occurrences always happen on the weekends? Both of the girls were sitting in the back seat of my car, safely seat belted and very content listening to nice, smooth Raffi on the CD player as we were driving home from somewhere. Could it have been swim class, Hebrew school, Girl Scouts, soccer, underwater basket weaving class (who the hell knows; they all run into each other, don't they?), when, out of the blue, Maggie said, "Mom?" And I of course had the brilliant comeback, "Yes, Maggie, what is it?" And she said with a huge sigh, "WELL, I just want you to know that I know that it's just not God who is making "those babies." She had started a few weeks earlier with this goofy little "snap and wink" thing, and so she did that to me.

Mollie looked at her and said, "Mommy, what is she talking about?" and I quickly said, "I don't know, Honey. But Mollie, when we get home, why don't you go over to the Wilsons' house to play with Michael and David? And Maggie, why don't you come into the bedroom so that you and I can talk?" I was thinking, "Oh no, I guess it's time for THAT talk!" When we got home, Mollie skipped down the street, oblivious to the fact that her mom was preparing to finally have "the talk" with her older sister and then to have a nervous breakdown (or just insert an I.V. of Tequila into her arm).

Maggie walked into the room with a smirky, Cheshire cat grin. I said, "OK, Honey, why don't you sit on the bed and tell me what exactly you were talking about in the car." Well, she looked at me with excitement in her eyes, as if she knew something that the whole, entire world was just waiting to hear. And she said, "Oh, Mom, I know now!" And I said, "OK, Honey, tell your Mommy what you 'know.'" And she said, "WELL,I know that the mommy has the egg and the daddy has the sperm, and when they kiss they can make a baby!" She was so excited that she had this big news flash. It was kind of like a "Quick, let's call CNN and talk to Wolf Blitzer right away" moment!

I didn't want to break her heart, and I did absolutely *love* the fact that she had prefaced her little "findings" with the "Mommy and Daddy" part (I wanted to give her that little snap and wink thing right back at her for that one). But, I just looked at her and in my kindest, most loving way possible said, "Oh, Maggie, you can't get pregnant by just kissing a boy."

She looked at me, puzzled, thought a while and said, "Well, then, where does the man's sperm come from?" I said, "Honey, the sperm comes from a man's penis." She then looked at me, and turned as pale as I've ever seen her (and this is a pretty pale kid to start with) and said "Oh, Mommy! Please don't tell me. . ." "Tell you what, Maggie?" I asked. She screamed, "Oh, Mommy, please don't tell me that I'm going to have to kiss a penis!" I then replied (and I have a feeling that I may have screamed at this point during our very mature conversation; tourists in Bermuda at the time could have heard), saying, "NOOOO, absolutely NOT!"

And then I added, very, very softly under my breath, "Only if you want jewelry."

Here is a recipe that might get you jewelry, also.

OYSTERS ROCKEFELLER

1 Tablespoon anchovy paste

1 Tablespoon anise seeds

2 Boxes of frozen chopped spinach, drained

½ Cup white wine

4 Sticks unsalted butter

5 Cloves garlic, minced

2 Shallots, minced

¾ Cup plain bread crumbs

½ Cup fennel bulb, chopped

2 Bunches of fresh parsley, chopped

2 Bunches of green onions, chopped

½ Cup of Pernod

*24 Raw, Atlantic oysters (and oyster shells if you happen to have them)**

½ Cup fresh Parmesan, shredded

Cook the frozen chopped spinach, and make sure you drain it very well (squeeze out all water). In a food processor, mince the garlic, shallots, and parsley. Add the fennel and green onions for a rough chop. Add anchovy paste, butter, wine and Pernod. Process just a few seconds to blend ingredients. Add the anise seeds and bread crumbs and blend for a few more seconds. Don't "over mix." You want this mixture to be fairly solid. Refrigerate mixture for at least 1 hour.

Place oysters on a baking sheet and add a dollop of the mixture on top of each. Sprinkle with Parmesan cheese and bake until the topping is brown and bubbly.

Serve with a good, simple, crusty bread – or even garlic bread to add more decadence.

*My family has been making Oysters Rockefeller for many years – and over time we have all accumulated our own stash of oyster shells. You can get your own by asking your new best friend at the seafood department in your grocery store if they would save some for you – or, if you are brave enough to buy and shuck your own oysters, you could start your own collection this way. Or, maybe make a phone call or pay a visit to a seafood restaurant and ask them for some shells. Make sure you clean the shells extremely well – you will need to boil them for at least 1/2 hour in saltwater. And also make sure you clean them well before each use. They will last for years.

If you do end up using oyster shells, line a cookie sheet with aluminum foil and spread a layer of small-sized rock salt evenly across the bottom of the pan. (You can buy rock salt at a hardware store.) Place the shells on top of the rock salt, place an oyster in the shell, and top with a dollop of sauce mixture. Bake the oysters until sauce is brown and bubbly.

Maybe instead of gems you'll get a few pearls.

Chapter 8

Don't You Just Hate When People Forget To Tell You The Little Details?

After I had Maggie, I was off work for the first time since I was 15 years old. Six glorious weeks. I've never ever been off that long. I had so many things planned. I was going to crochet a baby blanket, paint stars that shine in the dark in the baby's nursery, begin a baby scrapbook, do an in-depth diary of all of my innermost thoughts and feelings so that Maggie would know how much her Mommy loved her when I'm dead and gone, and the list went on and on.

Well, all of these plans were very well intentioned, but all I did for the first few weeks was stare at my beautiful baby, rock her in the leather rocking chair that Babs bought for us, have her lie on my chest and coo for hours (God, I love that phase), change a lot of poopy diapers, eat a lot of Heath Bar Cake, and walk around the house in an unbuttoned pajama shirt because I always wanted to be ready when the baby was ready to nurse.

I was the first person in my family to decide to nurse my baby. My Mom and sisters all thought I was nuts. I had waited 35 years to have this baby, and I wanted to make sure that I did everything in my power to make her as healthy as possible. I had already picked the worst person I could have ever thought of to be her biological father, so I thought the least I could do was to nurse her. I knew that I wasn't going to become the president of the La Leche League anytime soon and then nurse Maggie until she was 8 years old. Have you ever seen a woman who nursed her child when they were way out of the "baby phase"? Eek, I really don't want to offend any of my readers, but I always thought it was a bit creepy when a child is able to say, "Mommy, can I have a cookie with that tit?"

No, all I wanted to do was to make sure that I nursed my beautiful, big-headed baby girl for at least 21 days. That was, according to one of my best friends Suzy, all you have to do to make sure that your baby would have all of the mother's immune antibodies.

My problem was that I was kicked out of the hospital 24 hours after I began the "hoo hoo heeing."

Unfortunately, I had Maggie before they passed the law that made it mandatory for hospitals to allow mothers to stay for a minimum of two days after giving birth. Thank you for that, Bill Clinton. So, I was kicked out of the hospital so quickly, I didn't have the "nursing" staff come in to show me the appropriate way to nurse my baby. I just figured, hell, I'm a college graduate, I'm almost 40 years old, I can figure this out myself. As you will soon learn, apparently NOT!

As I was counting down the days until my 21 days of mandatory nursing had ended, marking them off my calendar in the kitchen one by one, another one of my best friends, Dawn, who lived about 2 hours away, called to check on me one afternoon when I was alone with Maggie and my Heath Bar Cake.

She said "Hi, Lou, how is it going? I had to call and check on you and the baby. How is the baby and how is the nursing coming along?" I said, "Hi, Dawn. Thanks so much for calling. How are you?" I continued to ramble, due to lack of any REM cycle whatsoever, and said, "Honestly, nursing isn't bad at all. The baby latches on perfectly! It's just getting her off that is really awful!"

"What do you mean, Lou?" Dawn asked. "Well, she never wants to let me go and it's gotten to the point that I have scabs on my nipples from pulling her off of me! I then continued, "It's really terribly painful. I don't know how you've done this for all of these years with your three kids! , I really give you so much credit. I guess I'm just a big wuss!"

She screamed, "OH, LOU! Didn't anyone ever show you how to just stick your little finger into the baby's mouth to release the hold she has on you? It's simple and painless!" I was like "No, no one ever told me how to *release* her from my breast!" Dawn just laughed and said "Oh, Lou, I'm soooo sorry. I just assumed you knew the basics."

Anyway, the moral of my story is that leaving out little details can be painful in so many different ways. Once I healed, I ended up nursing both my daughters until they were both around 1-1/2 years old. It was a wonderful experience— once I knew what the hell I was doing.

Here is another recipe I loved while I was nursing:

BAB'S STRAWBERRY JELL-O MOLD EXTRAORDINAIRE

Preheat oven to 350 degrees
2-1/4 Cups crushed pretzels
1-1/4 Cups melted butter
3 Tablespoons brown sugar

Mix together, then press into a 9 x 13 pan and bake at 350 degrees for 10 minutes.
Let cool.

8 oz. Cream cheese (let stand until soft)
1 Small tub of Cool Whip
1-1/4 Cup sugar

Mix cream cheese and sugar first and then fold in Cool Whip with electric mixer.
Spread over cooled pretzels.
Refrigerate.

1 Large pkg. strawberry Jell-O
2 Cups of boiling water
1 Pkg. frozen strawberries, thawed

Dissolve strawberry Jell-O in the boiling water. Add the frozen strawberries and pour evenly over refrigerated cream cheese mixture.

Refrigerate again and allow gelatin to set.

Enjoy!

Chapter 9

Guilt And The Art Of Putting It All In Proper Perspective

Why did it take me about 42 years to put everything I've been through into perspective? It took my two goofy little girls to finally make me see what's really important and what doesn't mean diddly squat in life. It would be the understatement of the millennium to say that I'm thankful for Maggie and Mollie for being a part of my life. When I'm not ready to put them in time out for about 3-1/2 years or thinking about inserting that I.V. of Tequila in my veins because of their continual fighting, I look at both of them and realize that they are the sole reason why I did what I did. I finally left P.D. and took the kids when they were very small— almost 3 and 5 years old. I was broke, and my credit rating (along with my nerves) was pretty darn shot.

Just prior to leaving the ex, I got a great new job, which I still have. But, with many new sales jobs, especially those that are 100 percent commission, there is always a struggle in the first year to make your quota and stay employed. What a concept! One person in the family should be employed, don't you think? That entire year, I was pretty much racked with guilt. After all, to him I was nothing more than a meal ticket. Lovely guy that he was, he often threatened to harm me and everyone I knew if I ever left. And in this horrible, raspy old disgusting voice with bad vodka breath, he would continually say that if I ever did leave, the next time I saw the girls "would be on a milk carton." He also said things like, "All I have to do is put a bullet in your left temple and no one will ever know." I hardly need to say that I was a nervous wreck all the time.

Have I mentioned that I'm Jewish? So, right there, you can add guilt to my mental state. I felt guilty for being a lousy mom who picked such a creep as the "Father of The Year" for my two little girls. Then there was "corporate guilt" for not being the perfect employee, because I was more than a little preoccupied. And then, of course, we have my "Family and Friends Guilt" (sounds like a cell phone plan, doesn't it?), because when P.D. was in his sadistic mode, he loved to harass and threaten all my friends and relatives. I even felt guilty for having left him when he was at his lowest. I ended up getting a horrible case of shingles from all the stress. In the back of my mind, I always knew that had I not married P.D. the second time, I would not have had my two daughters. That knowledge did alleviate a little of the guilt, but I still felt horrible for having chosen the worst possible person to be their biological father. (They did turn out to be very pretty, so, I guess he wasn't the worst choice on Earth — but pretty damned close!)

The fact that I had to work such long hours and travel during this tumultuous time almost killed me. P.D. reared his ugly head about 18 times a day. I had to call the County Police Department so many times that they stopped bothering to knock on our door and let themselves in. They would just walk into the house and help themselves to an ice-cold Fresca. It was only after he put about 40 holes in the walls of our small three-bedroom house that I decided to take the girls and hide out for a few days. (When I asked him why he would do that to the home his children lived in, his response was, "*Because I could*." So mature.)

It was when we returned to the house that the proverbial light bulb over my head flashed on. You see, Maggie and Mollie always sneaked into my bed at around 6 AM. It was always my favorite time of day because it was just us. No television, no telephones, no anything. Just me and my two little girls. I needed them more than you can imagine because I was feeling pretty darn low and vulnerable. But, early in the morning, we could spend about an hour talking, snuggling, and laughing before we started running around the house like idiots trying to get ready for the day.

Anyway, I have no idea what inspired me, but all of a sudden, as I had the girls on either side of me, I sat up and said, "Okay, Maggie and Mollie, Let's have an 'honest day.' If I could do anything at all to be a better mommy, what would it be?" Maggie, the more serious and clingy of the two, quickly replied "Just never leave me when I'm sick again, Mommy." I thought about the time when I had a very important sales call downtown. It resulted in a nice sale and about four house payments' worth of commission. I had gotten a call from Maggie's daycare that she had puked. I hurried from downtown (about a 30-minute drive), picked her up, took her to my mother's, and then went back downtown to close the sale. I looked at her, and of course I knew that she was talking about that day. I just looked into her eyes and said, "Okay, Maggie, you now have my promise that I will NEVER EVER leave you again when you're sick. Okay?" She looked back at me and nodded. We hugged each other tightly, and it was good that we had conducted this mature negotiation.

Then I looked at my almost-3-year-old. She has dark brown hair that, since she was about 2 years old, she has been able to put in this cute "high bun" on top of her head. She looked at me and I said, "Okay, Mollie, it's your turn. What can I do to be a better mommy for you? Tell me anything at all that I can do to be a better mommy." I swear, without one second of hesitation, this kid looks at me with her huge brown eyes, with this goofy bun on top of her head, in her Winnie-the-Pooh footy pajamas and said, "MORE BEEF." I was a little taken aback. "What? What kind of beef, honey?" And she said, once again, with no hesitation at all, "Oh, I don't know Mommy. . . . roast beef, corned beef, any kind of beef."

Well, that is when I found Perspective. Here I was so worried that I had totally screwed up my kids, that somehow they would both be on the Montel Williams show in about 14 years with tattoos and piercings, and all my kid wanted was a little more red meat. Perspective is an amazing thing.

What other recipe could I possibly do, but "beefy" MEATBALLS?

GRANDMA JOANIE'S FAMOUS MEATBALLS

Meatballs

1 lb. ground beef
1 teaspoon minced garlic
½ Cup Italian bread crumbs
3 Tablespoons Worcestershire sauce
2 Eggs
1 Cup chopped onions
1 Tablespoon parsley
Mix together and refrigerate for about an hour.
Fry ½ inch balls in vegetable oil until browned. Place them on paper towels to drain.

Sauce
1 Large jar of grape jelly
(2) 12-oz. jars of chili sauce
In a fondue pot or a medium-size sauce pan, mix the grape jelly with two 12-oz. jars of chili sauce.
Warm the sauce and carefully place the meatballs into the sauce.

Enjoy the beef!

Chapter 10

The Science Of Personality According To Laura Ray

I know that this is not rocket science, and I don't think that anyone will end up quoting me in the *New England Journal of Medicine* anytime soon. But one of the things that I've always found perplexing is the science of "personality." Let me just make a "scientific claim": it's a genetic crap shoot.

Even when you look at siblings, with the same mother and father and the same environment, they often end up being as different as night and day. A perfect example is my two sisters and one brother. They are all my best friends in the world, but we are totally different in every way except one. The one thing that we all have in common is our almost to a fault, on the verge of stupidity, generosity.

Unfortunately, we are all well known in a variety of circles. Restaurant servers and bartenders throughout the Midwest fight to wait on us. They know all four of us by name. Babysitters and cleaning women fight to service us, bellhops love our generous tips and trash men love our Christmas gifts. The list goes on and on, because they all know that we all tip and pay way over the standard. Gifts are to the point of stupidity. Chanukah, birthdays, graduation and so forth have gotten to the point that we all need to take out second mortgages to pay for them.

I remember when I was first married to P.D. and we were struggling financially (that's what happens when one partner decides not to make any money for several years, pretends to be employed, and hides out all day at local bars — another lesson learned). I finally realized how ludicrous it had become when I asked my niece, the daughter of my very generous and sweet oldest sister, what she wanted for her eighth birthday. I thought she was going to say, "Oh, Aunt Lou, I would love a Barbie doll, or maybe even a Cabbage Patch doll with a matching playhouse." Oh no, not one of our offspring. She quickly answered, "Well Aunt Lou, what I'd really like is a kayak." Can you even believe it? A freakin' kayak for an 8-year-old. Hell, she didn't even know how to ride a bike! Meanwhile, I couldn't pay the water bill or pay for daycare (because, of course, P.D. was at the bar all day while I was working). But, because my sister had been so wonderful and giving to me, I had to reciprocate to her child. So, what did I do? I found a beautiful used kayak and split the cost with another sibling. I tried to hide it for a while (the damn thing didn't fit in any of our closets). Then P.D. found it, screamed, and yelled that he was "sick and tired of [me] trying to buy everyone's love." He called me a lying [worst name you can think of], and then he stopped speaking to me for about a week (a huge blessing in disguise, now that I think back).

Here is what I think is the reason for all this insanity. Yes, you may call me Dr. Laura (not the one on the radio). I honestly think that all four of us subconsciously want to counter the stereotype that Jewish people are cheapskates. All four of us are middle class and are struggling like everyone else in the world, but we think it is our personal responsibility to change that image. It's not easy, but I guess we are trying to change the horrible misconception "one restaurant at a time."

I was a waitress for 10 years, all through high school and college (even for a time after college). That double degree really paid off, huh? I hated more than anything when I waited on someone and I knew they were Jewish and they tipped less than 20 percent — especially with my fantastic service. In my head I was always screaming, "Why, oh why could you not have been an Episcopalian or a Southern Baptist? Why the hell did you have to be Jewish?"

Our family's generosity comes in many forms. One of them is our ability to clean, help out, and especially cook in any time of crisis. When there is a death, sickness, move, coming-out party, whatever, we are all there with hundreds of Pyrex dishes filled with enough delicious homemade things to easily feed a small town in Beirut. For some reason, Jews are well known for cooking beef briskets. My sister was sweet enough to give me a wonderful recipe that was handed down by my favorite aunt. I have so many bottles of chili sauce, secret spices and onions on hand for this recipe — just in case. I had to design an entire section in our cupboard to hold all of them.

This brisket situation has gotten so bad that a few weeks ago I volunteered (as always) to cook for our daughter's swim team awards banquet.

Mollie and I woke up early to go to the butcher, who of course now knows us by name. We started cooking at around 7 AM (brisket takes forever to cook!), and when my husband woke up at 8 o'clock, stumbled into the kitchen to make our first cups of coffee and saw the briskets, he looked at Mollie and me and said, "*Oh, hell. Who died?*"

MY FAVORITE AUNT (AUNT GAIL) IN THE ENTIRE WORLD'S FAMOUS BRISKET RECIPE

1 Large aluminum foil pan (this type of meat really cooks so much better in an aluminum foil pan vs. a roasting pan)

5- to 6-lb. Beef brisket, with some fat
2 Bags of small red potatoes, washed clean
1 Medium yellow onion, chopped

Place brisket in aluminum pan with the fatty side up

Place small potatoes all around the brisket in the pan.

Generously season the brisket with Worcestershire sauce, Crazy Jane's Mix-up Salt (found in the supermarket spice aisle), garlic salt, Lawry's Salt, and table salt & pepper.

Pour 2 Jars of chili sauce on the brisket and potatoes and spread evenly.

Place the chopped onions on top of the brisket.

Wrap very tightly with heavy-duty aluminum foil and bake at 325 degrees for 4 to 5 hours.

The longer you cook it, the better it is.

I slice it (against the grain) after about 4 hours and then place it back into the pan and cover it again. Or, after it cools for a while, slice it against the grain, put it back into the gravy and serve it with dollar rolls.

Chapter 11

Someone's Dream Vacation

I ended up with the two best sisters-in-law in the world. I guess that old saying, "the third time is a charm," pertains to both my marriages and to the in-laws, because the first two (even though it was the same guy and the same in-laws), please pardon my French, really sucked! I'm sure that if you were to meet them, you would understand completely.

My new sisters-in-law are two wonderful Southern women who drove up to "Yankee territory." They are both scared to death to fly, so instead they opted to take a 2-1/2 day drive to meet probably the first divorced Jew with two kids they had ever met. They couldn't have been sweeter; and when they realized that their younger brother was happy, they did or said something to him. I don't know what it was, but within about 22 minutes of their leaving to drive back home, Sven proposed. Sheryl, the younger of the two, even drove back up to St. Louis by herself to babysit our two daughters for our honeymoon.

They both treat Maggie and Mollie as if they were their own grandchildren, and every summer the kids go down South for 2 weeks for what we have now named "Camp Sheryl." So, to say that I'm grateful to both of them for being so easy, open-minded, generous and loving is a huge understatement. I vowed to myself that I would repay their kindness whenever possible.

Well, the "repayment" came sooner than I had anticipated and therefore, so did the "vacation from Hell". Sheryl called one wintry

Sunday evening, and as we were just talking about everyday stuff, she told me that one of her biggest unfulfilled dreams was to go to Branson, Missouri, to see the Andy Williams Christmas show.

As I was walking toward my purse to write a check out so that she could do just that, she dropped the real bombshell. She said that it just wouldn't be complete if Sven, the two little high-maintenance girls and I didn't go with her and her husband.

All I was thinking was "Oh shit! Sven is going to kill me. My husband would hate nothing in the world more (other than perhaps putting bamboo shoots up his nail beds), than going to Branson, Missouri, the Succotash Capital of the world. The place where that sexy accessory called "the butt bag" was invented. I knew that telling my bluesy, "music snob of a husband" (he hates when I call him that) that we were going to take his sister, brother-in-law, and two little girls down to Branson for a weekend was not going to be pretty!

He looked at me with total disbelief and said, "You are kidding me, aren't you?" and then screamed, "You really didn't tell her that we would go, did you?" I rambled on and on about how important "family" is and how his sister had been so wonderful to us I don't know what else I said, but the next time I saw my loving, sweet husband, he was figuratively pounding his head against the wall .

The trip wasn't as horrible as I had anticipated. We waited in lines with thousands of women and their butt bags, stood for about 2 hours to eat at a restaurant where they actually threw rolls at your head (and you paid them for doing it!), and shelled out $42 admission for each of us to enter a crowded amusement park decorated with wall-to-wall Wal-Mart Christmas Lights and where the average age was 68 and the average weight was 268. I spent most of this time watching my husband look at me in disbelief.

That Saturday night, when we thought we couldn't possibly have more fun or excitement, we were able to purchase fifth-row seats to the "Andy Williams Christmas Show." It was everything you could hope for: the dancing reindeers, the schmaltzy 81-year-old Republican guy in a red and green plaid sweater whose name adorned the entire red velvet theater, the Lawrence Welk dancers, and of course, at the end, the abundant soap flakes that were supposed to resemble snow that fell on our heads. I kept looking at the faces of my sister- and brother-in-law and our two little girls and thought, "this isn't as bad as I thought it would be." But as soon as I felt that warm and fuzzy feeling, I caught a glimpse of Sven glaring at me, and said sheepishly to myself, "*Never mind.*"

After the show and a lovely dinner at a Lone Star Steak House, where I ordered a much-needed Margarita, I decided to have the lobster (don't ask me why — Sven still laughs about that). I guess that, after enduring the entire weekend, I thought I deserved the most expensive thing on the menu. I never do that; I guess I just felt like being a brat for an hour. Please note, in a city where the gourmet delicacies range from succotash to fried pickle on a stick, ordering a lobster at a 2-star steak house is not the most brilliant thing to do. It was probably one of the most disgusting dinners I've ever eaten; it was mushy and green. And because I was a waitress for more than half my life, I'm always embarrassed to send things back. Anyway, I ended up eating off our daughters' plates.

After the lovely dinner, we all went back to the Branson Comfort Inn ("Branson" and "comfort" in the same sentence — now there's an oxymoron). My sister- and brother-in-law went to their room, adjacent to ours, and the girls, Sven and I went to our two single beds. It was about 10 PM and the girls hit the bed and passed out. The excitement of the city just drained the girls, or could it have been 28 hours of non-stop fighting with each other, except of course during the star-studded theater show.

Of course, Sven and I couldn't fall asleep. But with the girls in the bed 6 inches away from us, we couldn't do anything else. I also think that we were also just too giddy from having our brains totally sucked out. Not having anything else to do, we decided, in the tradition of David Letterman, to make our own "Top Ten List" titled "Things You'll Never See in Branson." It got to the point while we were making our list that I was laughing so hard, tears were streaming down my face. I thought I was going to wet my pants (which would have been horrible since I was sharing a single bed with my hubby).

The list went something like this:

<u>The Top 10 Things You Will Never See in Branson</u>

Number 10 – An L.A. Weight Loss Clinic

Number 9 – A Jewish delicatessen or a synagogue (or a Buddhist temple or Mosque, for that matter)

Number 8 – A Jheri-Curl Salon

Number 7 – A public library

Number 6 – A chapter of MENSA

Number 5 – A gay bar

Number 4 – A Gold's Gym

Number 3 – A Health-food store

Number 2 – An inter-racial couple

AND THE #1 THING THAT YOU WILL NEVER FIND IN BRANSON (are you hearing the drum roll right about now....)

A 5-7-9 Shop

When all was said and done, we packed up the "fighting clown" children, the in-laws, and my thrilled-to-be-going-home Sven. As we were driving through the beautiful Ozark Mountains, my sister-in-law looked at me and said, "Thank you, Laura," "This was probably one of the best weekends of my entire life."

And that made the entire weekend worth it.

Here is one of my favorite recipes that you will not find anywhere in Branson!

SHRIMP LINGURIAN à la LOU

1 Pound of shrimp – cooked, peeled and deveined
½ Cup of olive oil
½ Cup (1 stick) butter
½ Teaspoon crushed red pepper
½ Teaspoon minced garlic
¾ Cup of quartered walnuts
½ Cup of rinsed julienne-cut sun-dried tomatoes (look for a jar in the Produce section of your supermarket, near the tomatoes)
Salt and pepper
¾ Cup of crumbled Feta cheese
1 pound of spinach fettuccini
1 pound of plain fettuccini

In a large pot, boil water with ½ tsp. of salt and 1 tsp. of olive oil.

Cook both packages of fettuccini until al dente, stirring so that the two pastas are mixed together.

When done (hopefully at the same time as the shrimp sauté), drain and put in a large, pretty pasta bowl.

At the same time, take large sauce pan, and over medium heat melt the butter and add olive oil. Add crushed red pepper, minced garlic, walnuts, and sun-dried tomatoes. Add salt and pepper to taste, and then add the cooked shrimp.

Sauté all ingredients until hot. At last minute, crumble the Feta cheese and stir it in very lightly so that it is slightly warm.

Pour all ingredients over the pasta and serve immediately.

Chapter 12

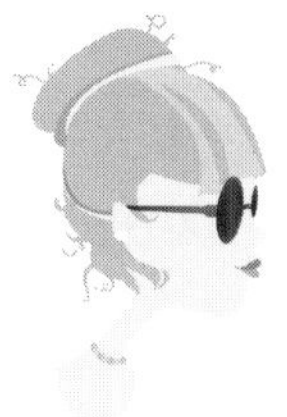

I Always Thought I Was Cute (Too Bad the Rest of the World Doesn't Agree)

Last month, Sven and I finally got to spend time at the house by ourselves. Sound the trumpets, blow the horns, don't tell *anyone* at all! We were so excited. It was the first time in 4 years, besides our honeymoon, of course, that we were without kids. My wonderful sister-in-law decided to open up "Camp Sheryl" (she invited the girls to stay at her house) The kids were really excited (but not quite as excited as we were). They spent 17 days pretending that they were "country kids," fishing, swimming in ponds, riding ATVs and not costing their Mom and Dad's $500 per week per child, as real camp would.

We dropped the kids off at the airport and I was a mess. Even though you spend an extra $100 per child to be babysat through the airport and I knew that it was as safe as it could possibly be, this was actually the first time that the girls ever went away to "camp," much less fly on an airplane by themselves. Airport security let me go through the airport with the girls. Sven had to stay at the $12 per cup Starbucks at the front of the airport. Once the nice flight attendant took the girls onto the plane, I just lost it and started to cry. All of a sudden a man came up to me, held my hand and said, "Lady, don't you know that you have to, "*let them go to let them grow*?" I feebly smiled at him, wiping away my tears and not even caring that mascara was running down my neck. I wasn't quite sure if I wanted to thank the man for his lovely advice or flip him off. Of course, I just smiled and didn't say a damn thing.

Sven and I drove home, each with totally different lovely thoughts in our mind. His, how we were going to have fun in bed for about 1-1/2 days and mine, how I was finally going to have a chance to clean out the girls' dresser drawers and get rid of all of their size 6X clothes. (Somehow it doesn't seem fair that they are growing normally but I went from a children's size 6X to a Women's size 12 with no in between at all.) Anyway, when we got home, Sven ran upstairs and put on some very sexy Marvin Gaye music, lit some candles, poured a Fresca (we are strange in that way — plus, it was only about 10 AM) and jumped into bed. I, on the other hand, ran upstairs, washed my face (because I looked like crap from 2-1/2 hours of crying), and quickly put on a semi-sexy nightgown. I've never been able to hook those damn garter belts. How do those people at Victoria's Secret expect you to turn around, bend over backwards and attach a tiny bit of delicate panty hose (that I usually "run" within seconds of getting them out of the package) and not fall over on your ass? Well, it wasn't pretty, but it was the best that it was going to get at 10 o'clock in the midst of a traumatic morning.

I jumped into bed and we had a lovely time. I was able to take my mind completely (well, almost completely) off the fact that our two little girls were on an airplane alone flying to Florida. Within seconds (it must be radar) of being able to lie in Sven's arms with that fabulous "P.C. Glow," (you can figure it out) the phone rang. I rolled over to pick it up while simultaneously listening to my husband screaming "NOOOO!" My sister was calling.

Of course I had to pick it up— she's my older sister. Who cares if I'm a grown woman with kids? I still am slightly (who am I kidding; I'm so much so that it's embarrassing) controlled by my older, bossier, opinionated, yet loves me to death sister. This is the time that one might want to ask themselves, "How old will I have to be when I stop caring what my mother, brother, trash man, or that cute guy who works in Frozen Foods thinks?" (That will be another chapter later on.) Having said that, though, honestly there is no one who controls me more than my older sister, Babs. I don't think I've told you much about Babs. She is fabulous, always "out there," and is universally loved by all. She has probably the best personality of anyone I've ever met. She's generous to a fault — until you piss her off, and then she can cut you off very quickly. That's really not her fault because in Numerology, I figured out that she is an 8 (see Chapter 7).

Babs has had about 27 times the boyfriends I ever did while

growing up. She's just always been a "man magnet." Even though my sister has struggled with her weight ever since I can remember, it has never stopped her from always dressing to the nines, always a million times more flamboyant than I. Add the gold lamé, feather boas, and sassy accessories along with her personality, and she always ends up being the center of attention in any situation. I've always wanted to have about just one-fiftieth of my sister's personality and her wonderful sense of self.

This particular day was not one of her finest. She definitely wasn't having the same "glow" I was experiencing at the time. She was actually crying hysterically, having had a huge fight with her husband. He ended up leaving and spending the weekend at their lake house, and she was alone in her beautiful big home in the city. Words just tend to vomit right out of my mouth (how charming) without me even thinking about the repercussions. But within milliseconds, I just blurted, "Babs, don't even think about it, I'll be right down. It will take me 20 minutes to pick up lunch and drive down to your house, and we can talk all afternoon." I wasn't going to give her a chance to say "Oh no, Sis, don't worry. I'll be fine and I know that you and Sven haven't had time in years to be alone."

I hung up the phone and looked at my darling P.C. husband, who was in fact looking at me as if I had totally lost my mind. He sat up, his eyes very wide, and said quite loudly and just a little on the "pissy" side, "Honey, what about round two?" What about our plans to drive in our ($2000, not very reliable) convertible up to the wine country?" He just kind of gave up, grabbed his pillow and turned over, while at the same time kind of muffled a, "Fine, just wake me up when you get back." And then, just as he was passing out and snoring sweetly, he was able to get out a "Love ya, Babe." God, I love him so much. He is always so sweet and easy on me. Even though he really doesn't "get it" when it comes to my neuroses with my family (for that matter, neither do I!), he'll never criticize me. Because of that, there will definitely be a "round two" and even a "round three" later on in the day after I help to settle this latest crisis (they really need me in D.C., don't you think?).

Within minutes, I was able to jump in the shower, get dressed, drive to one of our favorite fast-food restaurants, order one of everything on the screen, and drive to her house to help rescue my poor, verklempt (a Yiddish term for "really upset") sister.

I ran into her gorgeous home with about four bags of fast food. As we ate most of everything in all the bags, she was able to tell me the whole story. I listened, did my sisterly deed of telling her that she was "completely right" and he, of course, was wrong But of course not too wrong, because of course, for more than 20-something years, he's been a fabulous husband and father, and even though he had made a wrong judgment (not that horrible, I promise — but, don't tell her that I said that!), we decided to put on our swimsuits and swim off our little lunch.

It was then that my big sister, who had been distraught only 14 minutes ago, decided to drop the bomb in my lap. As we were lying on adjacent swim mats, she grabbed my hand lovingly. I looked at her like, "Oh shit, now what?" Still holding my hand, she said, "Louie" (did I tell you that my entire family and close friends call me either Lou, Little Lou, Louie, or Louis? And, by the way, I hate it when people I barely know call me by my pet name.). Anyway, she continued with, "I love you so much, Louie, and you do know that I think you're so beautiful." I began to get really afraid. "What the hell did you do, Babs?" I asked, feeling like I might upchuck the 2-1/2 bags of fast food that I had just consumed. She looked at me with a very sweet and reassuring smile and said, "Well, I just don't want you to be surprised if a camera crew from the show "What Not to Wear" kidnaps you in the next few weeks!"

I screamed, "What??" "You're kidding me, aren't you?" As sweetly as she could, still holding my hand tightly, she said, "Louie, don't worry! They give you $6,000 for a brand new wardrobe!"

So, I was thinking, "Oh yeah, that's okay, then. Don't worry about being f*!&ing humiliated on NATIONAL TELEVISION, having two fashion wannabes tell me what a loser I am and making me throw away all my old clothes (which I happen to really like). Don't worry about all that. "Little Louie" (now, I'm starting to really hate my nickname) will get enough money to buy about one-and-a-half outfits from some stupid designer store on Rodeo Drive. (If you ever want something that can kill a "P.C. glow" in a millisecond, this would be it.)

The most pathetic thing about the entire ordeal is that deep down, I think I'm pretty cute and fashionable. I guess the moral of this sad story is that apparently SHE DOESN'T! My big sister, the one who wears leather and pink feather boas (at the same time), wrote a plea to this cable network show to please help her "BIG FASHION LOSER" of a little sister. At that moment, I just wanted to slit my wrists. I wasn't sure if I wanted to laugh hysterically, cry, or strangle her! Probably, if I did all three simultaneously, it would be therapeutic.

So, once again, I screwed up. Here I had left the warm, romantic bed with my wonderful husband who thinks I'm pretty, spent about $45 on lunch, ran downtown to Babs's house, consumed enough calories to probably get me through Spring, all to be told that I'm going to have to dress incognito in a dark raincoat and dark sunglasses for the next few months because I'm probably being stalked, as I'm writing this, by a national camera crew who will let me know that they think I look horrible on national television. And of course this show is on a channel that re-runs each episode a minimum of 1,237 times.

OK, then — everything is just about status quo in the life of Laura Ray

This recipe has nothing at all to do with this story, it's just one of my all-time favorites that I got from one of my best friends/ favorite cousins (always interchangeable), and I always get a ton of compliments when I make it.

It's super easy and definitely great "comfort food." You can make it and enjoy it while I'll be "in hiding."

JAQUELINE'S DELICIOUS TIRAMISU

1 Bakery pound cake, fresh
¾ Cup cold brewed coffee
4 Tablespoons Kahlua
8 oz. Cream cheese – room temperature
1/3 Cup sugar
2 Tablespoons chocolate syrup
2 Tablespoons milk
Crushed Heath Bar or Skor dessert topping
Chocolate-covered coffee beans for garnish

Lay pound cake on its side. Cut the entire cake lengthwise into quarters.

Place the pieces side by side in a 9 x 13 glass baking dish.

Combine cold coffee and 3 tablespoons of Kahlua. Using a toothpick, poke holes in the cake.

Drizzle the mixture evenly over the entire cake.

With an electric mixer, beat together the cream cheese and sugar, then beat in the chocolate syrup, 1 tablespoon of Kahlua, and then the milk.

After the milk is mixed in, beat for about 1-1/2 minutes at high speed until the mixture is light and fluffy.

Spread cream cheese mixture over the pound cake.

Garnish with Heath Bar or Skor topping and chocolate-covered coffee beans.

Serve immediately or refrigerate.

Chapter 13

The Ugly Truth

As I have confessed before, I grew up in a pretty strange household. I guess, who hasn't? I hate people who pretend their families are allegedly "normal." Who the hell would even want to be? What does the word "normal" mean anyway? I've always thought that word was synonymous to boring. Maybe, just maybe, that's why I decided to marry P.D. twice… you think? Maybe a world filled with chaos and insecurity was my "comfort zone"… hmmm. Deep, isn't it? Hopefully by catching it early, a new generation (in a mere 40-50 years… but who's counting?) will stop the cycle of co-dependency and self-deprecating behavior. Laura Ray has a dream….

One thing that both of my parents were never big on was giving their children compliments. I'm not sure if this was on purpose. Were they trying to make each of their children little worker bees, always trying to gain the approval of their mother and father? I'm really not sure what their intentions were, but a possible by-product of it was that all four of us turned out to be pretty damn wonderful (if I do say so myself). My two sisters and brother are truly my best friends (although who isn't), and are all ambitious, successful in their own right, and generous to a fault (see Chapter 10 about big tips and beef briskets). We are all approval-seeking individuals who have always been prone to self-doubt and insecurity, especially moi (that's "me" in French), with the exception of about a three year period that quickly came to a halt one dark day in Jewish suburbialand. This dark day is the subject of this particular chapter.

I don't know when it all began, I just remember for the longest

Drunken Brie – Chapter 1

Unbelievably Delicious Blueberry Bars – Chapter 2

Key Lime Cow Pie – Chapter 3

Mediterranean Halibut for the Helluvit a la Gwendolyn - Chapter 4

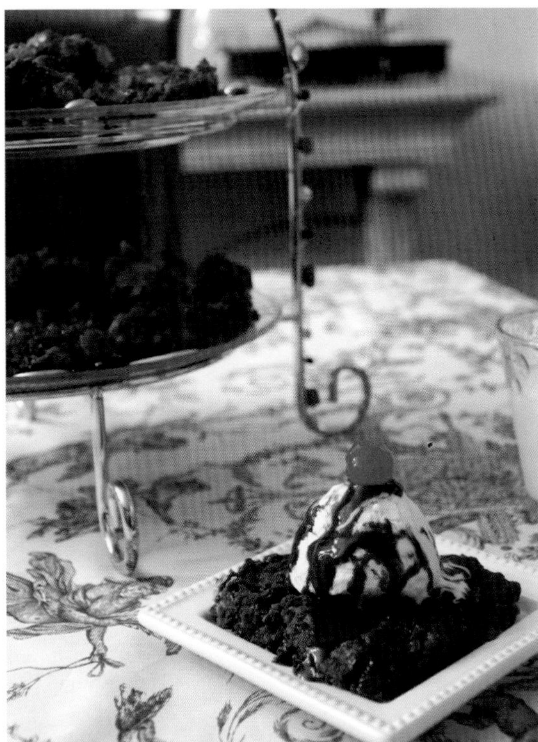

Helga's Orgasmic Brownies - Chapter 5

Grandma Betty's Delicious Heath Bar Cake - Chapter 6

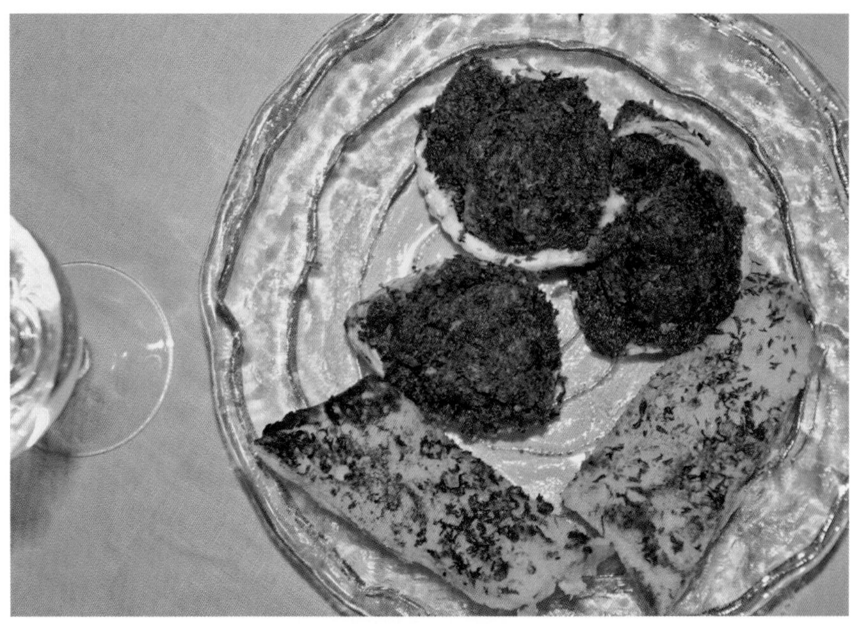

Oysters Rockefeller – Chapter 7

Bab's Strawberry Jello Mold Extraordinaire—Chapter 8

Grandma Joanie's "Beefy" Meatballs – Chapter 9

My Favorite Aunt (Aunt Gail) in the Entire World's Famous Brisket – Chapter 10

Shrimp Lingurian a la Lou – Chapter 11

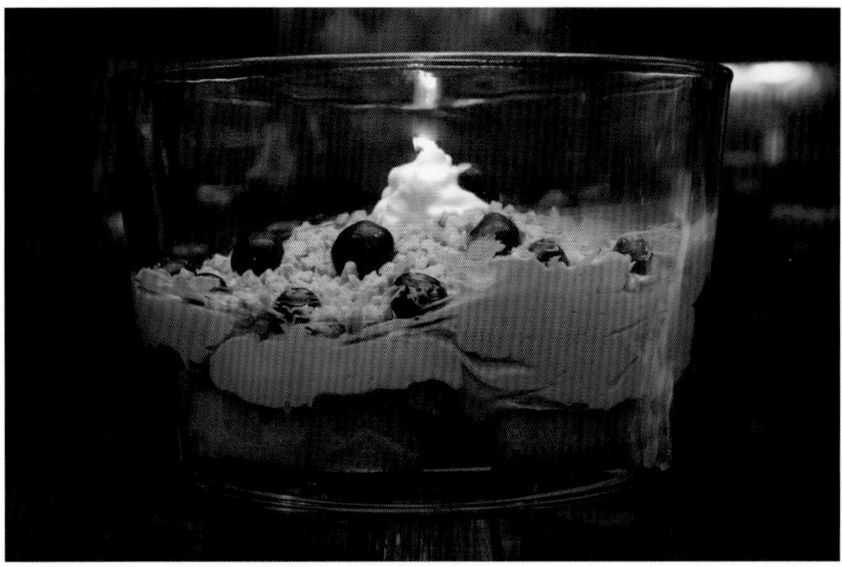

Jacqueline's Delicious Tiramisu – Chapter 12

Mama Mimi's Shrimp Dip—Chapter 13

Crab Stuffed Mushrooms - Chapter 15

Aunt Jutta's Noodle Kugel - Chapter 16

Sven's Crabcakes – Chapter 17

Bitty Ditty's Twice Baked Cheesy Potatoes - Chapter 18

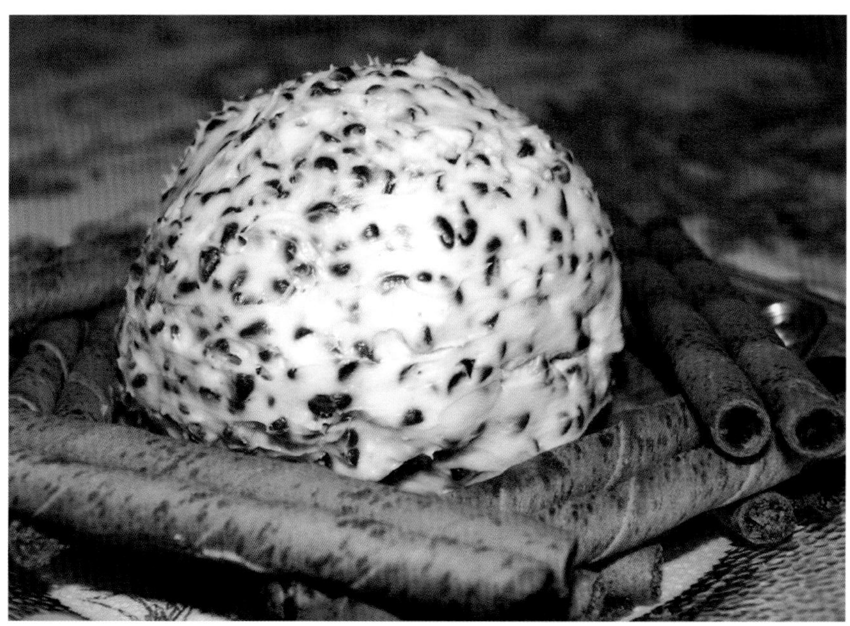

NBF Kimmie's Cream Cheese Ball - Chapter 19

Lola's Mushroom Dip - Chapter 20

Aunt Ethel's Oreo Balls - Chapter 21

Aunt Boo's Strawberry Pecan Salad - Chapter 22

Eggplant a la Lou Sue - Chapter 23

Chocolate Martini – Chapter 24

time (from about the time I was 5 or 6 years old), strange aunts and uncles would come out of nowhere and pinch the shit out of each of our cheeks, me especially. We came from a huge family. My Father once counted (must have been a slow day) and calculated that we had 268 second cousins. One by one, these cousins, aunts, and strange uncles (who have one eye about two centimeters higher than their other eye,hopefully not a genetic trait) would come up to me and scream (we come from a family of "screamers"), "Oy Vey Dalink (English translation – Oh My God, Darling), look at that! She is the spitting image of Bubba Rivva."

Who, may you ask is this infamous "Bubba Rivva?" Well, I had no clue who this woman was until literally hundreds, well maybe even thousands of relatives told me. Bubba Rivva was my Great Grandmother on my Father's side. She was my Zeyda's Mother. To the non-Jewish, non-Yiddish readers out there, Zeyda is Yiddish for Grandfather. To digress a bit, I always thought that my grandfather's first name was indeed Zeyda. We always called my other (maternal) grandfather "Oss" (his name was Oscar), so I just thought that Zeyda was indeed Zeyda Roodman and my other grandfather's name was Oscar Stein. It is actually pretty sad and shows how genuinely slow I am, because I was actually under this misconception until sometime in my 30's!

Well, with all of these strange people always paying me this huge compliment – looking just like Bubba Rivva, I thought I was pretty damn hot. No matter that at 13 years of age, I weighed a whopping 86 pounds, had bucked teeth so badly that I could literally stick my entire thumb in between my two front teeth, and had wavy, dirty blonde hair that always looked greasy because I was determined to have straight Peggy Lipton of Mod Squad fame styled long straight hair parted in the middle. In order to try to make it look like hers (who was I kidding?), I would constantly wet it, which in turn would make it look like I hadn't washed it for weeks.

I actually thought I had a close bond with my Zeyda. Not only was I the spitting image of his mother, but I was also the one who would spend hours upon hours playing gin rummy with him. This was after, of course, I had made him 2 to 4 "fingers" of Scotch every few hours after say, 10 a.m. A strange talent I know, but honestly, I was a damn good bartender at 13 years old and hell, by about 11:30 a.m. I always ended up beating him… I wonder why?!?

Things were going swimmingly. Life was surprisingly normal in our strange household until one day several years later, I think it was early Fall. I actually remember it like yesterday. Our Uncle Harry had passed away. Don't ask me who he was, what he did, or anything tough like that, as I had and have no idea. All I know is that our Father made us all go to sit shiva for good old Uncle Harry. If, of course, you don't know what the hell shiva is, it's simply like a Jewish wake. But instead of non-stop drinking like our fun Catholic friends; we tell stories about the departed and eat, and eat, and eat. The very good Jews eat and eat and eat for 7 days; our family always sits shiva for the minimum of three days (just enough to tilt the scale a good ten pounds).

I was minding my own business sitting with my sister Gwendolyn and my brother Johnny. Babs was lucky enough to have been out of town that Fall day and must have received a *Get Out of Shiva Free Card*. We had all just finished our second or third plate of pastrami and corned beef sandwiches, knishes, slaw, noodle kugel, etc. etc. etc., and all of a sudden one of our very loud aunts ran up to us, and said "You three, come with me, I have to show you something I don't think you've ever seen before!!!" She was so excited. I wasn't sure what she was going to show us. Could it have been that Uncle Harry had all ready risen from the dead? Could Barbara Streisand have realized that she was among our 268 second cousins and wanted to partake in some really good pastrami? I had no idea.

This aunt ran down a gloomy corridor and pointed at a huge framed picture of a woman. It looked like it was from some time in the middle 18th Century. Actually it was a portrait of a 235-pound hunchbacked, very sad looking woman with a unibrow (you know, one of those long, continuous bushy eyebrows that doesn't stop in between your two eyes). She was hunched over and so heavy that there was no comprehensible way of telling where her thigh ended and her ankles began. What I couldn't get out of my mind (still can't, can you tell?) was this huge mole in the middle of her chin with what looked like the longest, thickest, blackest hair growing out of it. She was wearing the most God-awful ugly black and gray knapsack with an even uglier schmatta on her head (aka: head covering) and looked as though she hadn't smiled in her entire life. Johnny, Gwendolyn and I just looked at this poor, poor woman, and said "Oh....Aunt Genevieve, who is this poor woman?" She looked at us and without pausing, she said, "That's Bubba Rivva."

I'm not really sure how it happened, but I looked in horror and screamed the most blood-curdling scream you could ever imagine. Actually, I heard years later, that the entire family thought that I was still in shock over the death of poor Uncle Harry and that's why I screamed. I was pale as a ghost and said, "Oh my God!!!! THAT'S BUBBA RIVVA?!?! That's the woman who could have been my identical twin?!?

I wasn't quite sure if I wanted to cry, faint, or puke up my pastrami. I looked at Johnny and my sister Gwendolyn, and they both looked at me, and in unison, they both started laughing hysterically. I remember that they were laughing so hard, Johnny had tears streaming down his face while Gwendolyn laughed so hard she wet her pants (which actually is not a very "shiva" kind of thing to do when you think about it). They were both rolling on the floor. Complete strangers looked at them and probably thought, "Oh my God, all of those Roodman kids are taking Harry's death so hard! Look at them, they are all in a state of hysteria!"

For almost an entire decade, until this horrendous night, I was thinking, "Oh...all of my relatives think that I look like this gorgeous Russian Jewish immigrant. My romantic vision of Bubba Rivva was a blend between Anna Kornikova and the Countess of Monte Cristo, who came to this country without a dime, but with her beautiful natural features, ended up with a wonderful life. Where in reality, all of these keen, and apparently semi-blind and disturbed, relatives saw me as an identical twin to a homely, unibrowed, "Babuschka'd-Schlubby-Bubby" (try saying that 10 times!). Instantly, my already acutely fragile self-esteem went completely out the window.

Years later, I'm not sure where that portrait went. I guess it should have been willed to her mini-me. I'm over the shock of it all now... it did take about 8 years of therapy and many co-pays to wipe away the image of her from my mind. Honestly though, I just don't think I'd be able to see pictures of this woman on a regular basis (even though I'm sure she was a sweet, generous, woman... wouldn't she have to be?)

Every once in a while, I do still find myself looking in the mirror, checking my chin to see if the hairs and moles have begun to surface.

The recipe for this chapter is from Gwendolyn's wonderful mother in law. We all call her "Mama Mimi." Hope you like it.

This recipe also has nothing to do with this chapter. Sven just likes it a lot. And I'm sure Bubba Rivva would have, too.

MAMA MIMI'S SHRIMP DIP

Mix together the following:
½ Bottle of chili sauce
1 Can of shrimp (or chop peeled and deveined shrimp into tiny pieces – about 1 cup)
8 oz. Cream cheese
5 Tablespoons of chopped onion
16 oz. Sour cream

Mix together, refrigerate for at least an hour, and serve with your favorite gourmet crackers.

Chapter 14

The Moment I Realized That I Had Lost Control Of My Life

Have you ever had that *aha* moment when you realized that something has got to change, because if it doesn't, you may have to be locked in some kind of rubber-walled room in the very near future? Well, such is the subject of this chapter. Once again, pretty damn embarrassing, but so true and disturbing (in a funny way, of course). (True, funny, disturbing — words that I'm using often in this book, have you noticed?)

Once upon a time, there was a bleached-blonde idiot who must have seen *The Sound of Music* one too many times. She thought that marrying a man with five kids would be one fun-loving adventure after another, where the beautiful children would love her, she would automatically love them back, and everything would be wonderful. In fact, not only would it be an ongoing love-fest, but she would eventually learn how to make all their clothes out of drapes, just like it was done in the movie!

I truly believed that marrying P.D., taking care of all his kids, and moving to backwards "South Bumblef@*&" was my twisted way of fulfilling my old desire to join the Peace Corps. You know, instead of living in the jungles of Africa, teaching children who survive on nothing and have to live off the land and who have no means to an education that would result in any kind of future, I, Laura Ray, could kind of do the same thing, but without having to pump my body with mega doses of antibiotics and go without a blow dryer for 3 years. I also wouldn't have to worry about any bugs or spiders that are bigger than our 15-lb. Chihuahua. I would still be saving a village (well, sort of — this would be a river town in rural Illinois, but a place that was in dire need of help, nonetheless).

You also must remember that I was a very immature and naïve 24-year-old who was intent on making a difference in our world. What a joke!

Anyway, my dream world started to unravel faster than imaginable. As I've said in previous chapters, probably ad nausem, right after I married him, Dick White morphed quickly into Dick Black, his drinking accelerated beyond the speed of sound, and his 15-year-old daughter (#2) had a baby. This, to me, was unfathomable, primarily because just a year before she got pregnant, I had stood in line for 3 hours at the only Wal-Mart in South Bumblef@#& to get her a Cabbage Patch Doll for Christmas. In those days, women went insane for those God-awful ugly dolls. Don't ask me, I was just doing my duty in my own little Laura Ray Peace Corps.

Looking back, I think I just sleepwalked through the entire decade, trying to do my best and help his kids the best I could through one disaster after another. And there were many: babies, drugs, boyfriends with the names like "Boney," hospitalizations, juvenile detention, flunking out of school . . . .You know, just all your run-of-the-mill episodes of "The Sound of Music... IN HELL". I often felt like I was that object in the Space Invaders game that constantly had to move back and forth to avoid being hit on the head and ultimately destroyed.

The most difficult thing about my little hell was that all of P.D.'s kids had a mother who was very much in the picture, living only blocks from our house.

So here comes my advice to all my friends (that would be you), and it comes straight from my heart. It goes like this:

Dear Friend,

Should you ever find yourself falling in love with a man with small children, please, for your own good, DO NOT marry him unless the children's biological mother is dead.

Sincerely yours,

Laura Ray

I know that sounds harsh, but I found out the hard way that trying to have any impact whatsoever with a kid, especially a daughter whose bond with her mother is so close, is completely, unequivocably impossible if the "real" mother is in the picture at all (unless of course, the "picture" on the wall is of the beloved dead Mom).

To try to instill your morals and values to any kid, no matter how much your effort, how much you love them, how much time you spend with them, or how many thousands of dollars you end up spending, will not do any good at all when Mom is out there sabotaging every bit of good you're trying to accomplish. Am I sounding bitter? Hopefully not, but I would have to be as saintly as Mother Teresa to not be bitter about the crap I went through. And honestly, I think that is why my mind just shut off and repressed hundreds of these bad experiences. I don't even think I've told Sven half the stories, to which I'm simply going to bestow the name, "As the Shit Turns." How about if I equate it to someone so involved in a cult, like being a Moonie or Hare Krishna (bet you haven't heard those names forever. I wonder if any of them are left?) Or maybe it was just that I was completely addicted to chaos. Whatever the hell it was, I always felt as though I was drowning in shit, and it was all due to the fact that I had made my vows, which I took very seriously, both to my husband and to these girls. I didn't think I would ever give up on any of them (stupid, but true).

Two years later, my stepdaughter finally got out of South B.F. Her baby was being taken care of by the biological father (who was 20 years old at the time and had become a roofer in his dad's business — a very reputable and good-paying job in South B.F.). And even though the past 2 years were very tough for her (She had to deal with small town high school mean girls, and it was much worst in the late 80s). She also experienced depression, being way too young to have to take care of a baby). I was so damn proud of her for going away to college to pursue her dream to be an actress.

My marriage was horrible. Thankfully, although I was living about 2 hours away from South B.F., I went back to my old job. My boss was so excited for me to come back that the company paid for a nice, furnished apartment for me to live in. They paid me $45 each day for food, put me up in a $1,500/month apartment, and gave me a new lease on life away from P.D. Sometimes even Corporate America can have a heart! Anyway, I drove home every weekend, whether I wanted to or not, and because I was the only one working at the time (an ongoing theme in our marriage), Dick didn't give me too much grief over it.

My stepdaughter was starring in her first college play. It was amazing that she had gotten the lead. I was beaming with so much pride, you could see "the glow" radiating from my head a mile away. There was no way in hell that I was going to miss her first performance.

So I took half the day off from work, drove 2 hours to pick up P.D. (I didn't trust him to drive), and then drove to the small college town, which was another 3 hours away. I had made dinner reservations for us and all her castmates. I knew we couldn't afford it, but I just put the entire bill on my corporate American Express and thought that I'd just worry about it next month (another recurring theme).

After dinner, we walked into the gorgeous theater, and I was carrying two dozen beautiful roses for the star of the play. I'm waving to everyone in the theater, trying to be politically correct, yet gentle, kind of like those pageant women do, basically just trying to let every person in the theater know that I was the stepmother of the play's lead and that we were so damn proud of her!

We were able to sit in the second row center, and I just couldn't contain myself. The play was completely sold out for opening night. By the time the red velvet curtain came up, every single person in that theater knew that we were the very proud parents. The theater went dark, the curtain came up, the lights went on and out walked my stepdaughter. She looked beautiful, but I did notice a new dragon tattoo on her arm. Wishfully I thought that this was just a temporary one, painted on for the sake of the play. Of course, I found out later that it was NOT. She was by herself in front of the sold-out crowd, and the first words that came out of her mouth were — I kid you not — were… "I love the taste of c**...it reminds me of my high school prom."

Honestly, if someone would just give me a shot glass of strichnine at that point, I would have finished it off neat. That would have been less painful. I wanted to literally crawl under my seat (actually, it's all a blur, but I think that's exactly what I did). Every damn person in the place knew that this kid was ours. P.D. was actually too drunk to realize what his daughter had just said, but unfortunately, I was completely sober. It was at this point in my life that I realized that things had to change. I had lost total control of my existence, and if things didn't change immediately, you would find me to be content in a rubber-walled room, bouncing back and forth for days on end.

By the way, this is going to be the only chapter in this book that doesn't have a recipe that goes with it... I couldn't think of one for the life of me that went with it... thank God!

Chapter 15

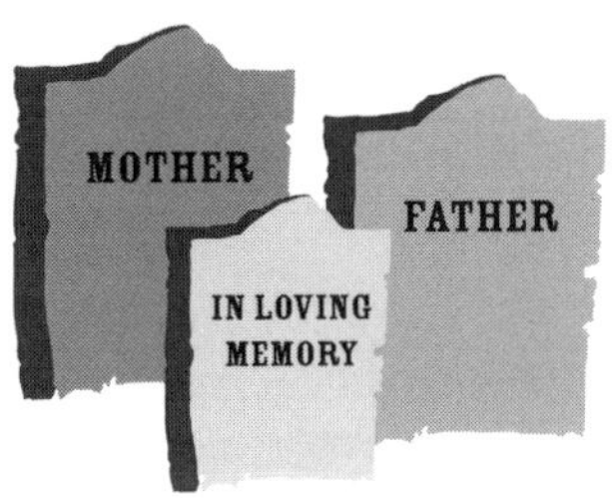

Sometimes It's Good To Be The Loser

Several weeks ago, don't ask me why, I got into a twisted contest with one of my other "working mom" dear friends whose life has been about as strange as mine. That's a little scary. Sometimes, we even play a game called "*Whose Life is Stranger?*" Everyone needs something to do in their spare time, don't you think?

I was having an absolutely horrible day. Everything that could possibly have gone wrong did. I had about eleven sales appointments, and I wonder if the stars were aligned in a bad way that made every single person I called on decide to be really mean to me. I guess it was my day to be the Sioux Indian on the day of "Half-Moon Rising of Sadistic Behavior" (I just made that up, could you tell?). Or maybe everyone just decided that I had the word *schmuck* tattooed on my forehead and they all decided to take out all their frustrations out on their handy sales representative.

Worst of all, I hadn't had time to eat a thing all day, and that is the one thing that can make me horribly bitchy and so self-pitying that it's unbearable. To top it off, during one of these encounters, I had to pee so badly that it was painful to even look outside at the pouring rain.

It was about 5:53 PM. This meant that I had about 7 minutes to pick up Mollie from the afterschool "latch-key program". If I didn't pick her up by 6:00 PM, not only would they charge me $1 for each minute that I was late, but much worse than that, all the daycare workers (who can't wait to go home) would look at me as if I were *The Mother From Hell.* Mollie would be the last kid at school, staring out of the window with her big brown eyes looking like "Little Orphan Mollie" waiting for a parent, any parent at all to claim her. *Could someone please just kill me now?*

I wasn't even close to school. To add insult to injury, the state transportation department (with all their great wisdom and about a $4 billion budget) had closed the one of three major highways in our city for 18 months. The one that was closed, of course, was the one closest to our home and the one that connects us from our home to all the places I had to go every single day of my life: to work, shop, and school. (and go to much-needed therapy. . . .Nah. I just added the therapy part for comic relief. The truth is that even though I needed therapy badly, who the hell has the time for it?)

So with the highway being closed for 18 months, I had to maneuver around on every damned side road to drive back and forth to work, along with about 1.2 million other really pissed-off people. This has added at least 2 hours each day in the car, and trying to make it to school on time on this particular horrible rainy day would take an act of God. Being the brilliant woman that I am and knowing that my situation didn't really warrant a miracle, I wasn't expecting an act of God anytime soon. Instead, I decided that I had better call Sven to see if he was closer to school than I was.

Just as I picked up the phone to call him, the phone rang. It was my friend Lilly, the one I mentioned at the beginning of this story. She started the conversation, not with a "Hi, Lou. How are you?" or a "What's going on?" No, without hesitation she began with, "Okay, you can congratulate me, Lou! I won the prize today for the world's shittiest day." I replied quickly, "Oh, I don't know, Lilly. Don't be too cocky about that. It's going to be a tough competition today, trust me!" "All right then, if you're going to play tough," she countered, "Let me just tell you what happened to me today, and then you can tell me honestly who won this twisted contest of yours." "Okay, go for it," I replied sweetly, knowing perfectly well that I would beat any story of hers to hell.

She went on, saying, "Well, I had to drive about 227 miles to the smallest tiny town in the bootheel of Missouri to try and sell an ad in Podunkville USA's local yellow pages to a man who owns a monument company. After about an hour and a half, he decided to splurge and buy about a $36 per month ad. I ended up making about $11.96 after taxes for the big sale. Then he made me draw up several ads that he pondered over, had his wife and three kids look at all of them to decide which one he wanted. They finally agreed on one, he signed the contract and I finally got to leave his place knowing that I wouldn't get home until about 9:30 PM tonight."

She continued with her sad saga, "When I pulled out of his small parking lot, I heard a crash! I quickly got out of my car and you won't believe what I saw!" I finally mustered some sympathy in my voice and said, "Oh please, Lilly, don't tell me…", and she said quietly, "Oh yes, I hit a tombstone!" "Oh no, I can't believe it!" I said, trying to make her feel better about it. "Lou, it gets much worse. When I hit the first one, it fell on another one, and then that one fell on another, and by the way, have you ever played dominoes?" "Oh Nooooo….," I screamed. "Oh Yes. Not only did I break one, but by the last count, I had broken six huge tombstones!"

Then, speaking in a strange, manic way, as though she was reliving this horrible experience. "I went back into that creepy old office to tell the owner what I had done and you know what he was doing?" "What, Lilly?" I asked, because by then I was feeling really sorry for her. "The guy was on the phone with the Podunkville USA Police Department telling them what I had done. I think the ass*&%@ thought that I was going to do the old "Hit the Tombstone and Run" thing!" I told him "Sir, I was not going to hit and run. I wanted to come in and apologize and pay for what I had broken. I would never do anything like that. Here, let me write you a check." So here I was, about to write a check for $150 for all of the broken rocks, everything I had in my checking account, and the guy looked at me and shook his head and said, "Well, that's fine, Missy. You can write me a check, but that check better be for about $6,800. I almost fainted, Lou."

At that point of the story, I was laughing hysterically and yes, I did finally pee in my pants. I said, "Oh Lilly, it's not that bad. Christmas is right around the corner and next year, you can just give all of us beautiful granite coffee tables. All you have to do is just put the side of the granite that says "In Loving Memory" or "Mother" on the back side, and no one will know!" Tears were streaming down my face. I could not have stopped laughing if I had tried. She then said, very somberly, and ignoring my hysterical laughter, "Well, I didn't even think of that. Hell, if my insurance company or I have to pay, I'm going to bring those tombstones home with me." She followed up with, "Shit — I'd better turn around on this two-lane highway and go back to gather my granite!"

I then paused for just a second as I was catching my breath and said "Lilly, guess what?". She said, "What Lou?"

I then said, in a very soft voice, "About the contest, Lilly. Guess What? YOU WON!"

This recipe is something great to serve on a coffee table (granite or not)

CRAB-STUFFED MUSHROOMS

12 Large mushroom caps, Stems Removed
1 Cup of dry white wine
8oz. Cream cheese (room temperature)
½ Cup Parmesan cheese
4 oz. Lump crabmeat
2 Teaspoons of Sherry
1 Tablespoon finely diced green onion
1 Teaspoon Worcestershire sauce
1 Teaspoon hot pepper sauce
½ Teaspoon ground black pepper
1 Teaspoon fresh lemon juice

Preheat oven 400 degrees.

Place mushrooms and wine in a small sauté pan and cook over medium heat for 5 to 7 minutes.

Remove mushrooms and carefully press out excess moisture between paper towels.

Set aside to cool.

In a large bowl, combine cream cheese, ¼ cup of grated Parmesan cheese, Sherry, onion, seasonings, and lemon juice. Mix well and then gently fold in crabmeat.

Stuff Mushrooms and top with the rest of the Parmesan cheese (1/4 cup).

Place on a cookie sheet and bake on the middle oven rack for 20 to 25 minutes, or until golden and bubbling.

Let cool slightly and serve.

Chapter 16

Three Funerals and a Brand New Lou

All right, if you don't think I'm strange after reading fifteen chapters, let me give you a little more proof.

I've decided that my entire outlook on life has changed. No, it's not from finally getting out of an abusive marriage, marrying the same jerk twice, having two high-strung daughters, having a demanding job, finally finding the love of my life at age 44. Nope, none of that. So you ask, "Okay, Lou, what has changed your life?" My reply would be, "Going to funerals." Yep, that's what has changed my life. I've been to way too many funerals in the last year, but three funerals that I had to attend in the last few months have totally changed me and my entire outlook on life.

Now I am starting to ponder bizarre things like, "I wonder how many people will actually show up to mine? Will any of my five old boyfriends show up? My favorite fifth-grade teacher (if she's still alive)? I wonder what kind of food will be served afterward, and will there be enough? (Who am I kidding? Of course there will be enough—We're Jews!) What will my husband wear? Will he wear one of his jazzy jackets, or will he wear a subdued black on black on black on black thing?" Twisted stuff like that. Do you think I may just have too much free time on my hands, or what? By the way, what the heck is with all this cancer going on? It's getting very scary.

Anyway, the first funeral that changed me was for Sven's friend. Let's call him "Bill." To even call him a friend is "poetic license." He was a 52-year-old guy whom Sven had done music business with and known for years. The word out on the street had it that Bill was actually so upset with Sven's closest friend, a man who is probably one of the kindest men I've ever met, he had actually put a "hit" out on him.

We don't even live close to New Jersey and no one I know has any resemblance to Tony Soprano whatsoever, so of course this story was just completely unbelievable to me. I just thought that everyone was just making it up because (a) they watched too much HBO and (b) it was a very slow news year. I also thought, "Man, does this Bill guy have a temper, or what?" None of Sven's friends or co-workers seemed to like this guy. Being the "glass half-full" kind of gal, I wanted to give this guy the benefit of the doubt. That doubt seemed to vanish a few seconds after I met him. About a month after I had married Sven, I met Bill for the first time. After talking with him for about 5 minutes (it had seemed like an hour and a half), he had asked my husband if he had lost his mind by marrying a woman with two young children. The man quickly lost all my affection. And let me just add that when Sven married me, the girls were 6 and 8 and were so much cuter, sweeter and a hell of a lot less hormonal than they are now. People were always commenting how lucky he had been for having us as a family. Today, when the kids' heads spin around and green goo spews from their mouths, it's always helpful to keep reminding myself of those less complicated, sweeter times.

Anyway, that was all I really knew about this man. Except, when I found out that he had suddenly died at the very young age of 52, I suddenly felt very sorry for a guy who had never found his true love, never had the joy of fatherhood, never knew what it was like to have true friendships (without putting "hits out" on them. *You know, those little details.*).

I then talked my husband and his best friend into going to Bill's funeral. Sven's friend said, "Hell, the asshole put a hit out on me for no reason at all, why would I want to pay my respects?" He actually had a very good point, but of course, the obnoxious salesperson that I am had to make the pitch. It was something like this: "Deep down, he must have been a good person, and you really should show your respect…blah, blah, blah." Thank God I talked them into going with me. With us, it made a whopping 22 people who came to the funeral. I felt so bad for the family that the turn-out was so horrible.

Here I was, a woman whom he didn't particularly care for, and I ended up cooking all the food for the shiva after the funeral. I didn't even know this guy, and here I was making brisket (you already have this recipe), my Aunt Jutta's famous noodle kuegel (you'll get this recipe), and a ton of other dishes. It was so bad that I barely had enough Pyrex dishes for it all (which is saying a whole lot!). I don't know why, but something was just drawing me to this poor guy's funeral and I felt like I had to help out.

It was a horribly rainy day at this terribly "icky" little cemetery (I guess none of them are wonderful.). As I said before, only about 22 people showed up. I even counted them and hoped a few were in the bathroom. (Who was I kidding? There were no restrooms at this cemetery.) How totally sad is that? Not that Bill deserved a parade or police escort; but hell, I had more people at our 14-pound Chihuahua's birthday party (the only reason why I had the nerve to have it was that Sven was on a business trip and the kids had invited all the dogs in the neighborhood, along with their owners, without asking me).

What made this funeral even more depressing was that Bill's mother (who was suffering from Alzheimer's) spoke in a loud voice throughout the short service, saying things like, "Doesn't look like there are many people here. I guess Bill didn't have many friends?" and all sorts of sad things like that. The few people who were there were all very uncomfortable, looking down at the ground to avoid eye contact with anyone. I just stood there in the rain crying for this poor guy who I didn't even like and for whom I had stayed up the entire night before cooking. It was all a *Come to God* moment that I definitely will never forget. My Mom used to drill into my sisters, my brother Johnny, and me the saying, "You have to be a friend in order to have a friend," over and over again. I wish she had known Bill.

The second funeral that changed my life was one for the dear father of another of Sven's friend. This man had lived a beautiful life and had three sons who loved their dad so much that it was painful and sweet at the same time, hearing each one of them speak of their fabulous dad. "Johnny Diamond" (Sven's friend and the oldest of the three brothers) stood at the pulpit and eloquently told a story about his father. He said that when he was a young kid, his dad would wake up at 5 AM every Saturday morning, even though he had to go to his jewelry store at 10 AM and work until 8:00 o'clock that evening. He would do this so that he could drive his son to baseball practice located about an hour away from where they lived. Johnny said that, for years, he would sit in the front seat and moan and groan, complain, and just make it miserable for his father as he was driving him to practice. Finally, when he was a teen, Johnny looked at his dad while he was driving, who during all of these years had never said a word, never complained about having to wake up early on the only day that he could sleep in until 8 AM had it not been for his son's baseball practice, and said "Dad, why do you put up with me being such an ungrateful jerk every Saturday morning?"

His father looked at him and softly said, at 6:15 in the morning, when it was still dark outside, "Son, I've done this every week for the last 6 years so that when you're a father, you will do the same exact things for your children." Very simple and beautifully said. I think all of us parents do that without even thinking about it, but as soon as I got home from this moving service, I came home and told my two daughters the same thing. Maybe, they will remember it and pay it forward. Then again, maybe not!

The last funeral that changed me forever was the most horrible. I will just very briefly describe it because it was painful beyond words. A cousin of one of my best friends (she's been one of my best friends since I was 10 years old) had a 20-year-old son who was beautiful inside and out. Andrew had just finished his junior year in college and decided to drive 1,200 miles home to begin his summer break and get a job in town until he went back for his senior year at school. Even though his dad urged him to let him fly to New York so that he could drive with him, he decided that it would be a welcome time to drive by himself and do some soul searching. On some small stretch of the highway in the middle of nowhere, he fell asleep at the wheel, ran his car off the road, and died instantly.

This funeral was so heart wrenching that I actually am crying as I am writing this, remembering the details. Most of it is a blur. The congregation was so packed that there were even people standing outside to show their respect. There are absolutely no words that you can say during a time like this. It just makes you think what parents go through when they find out that their child has been killed in war or has a terminal illness. This family has been destroyed. There is nothing you can do, no number of briskets that you can make, no flower arrangement that can be purchased, no amount of money that can be donated that can even begin to fill the hole in their lives.

I drove home by myself that afternoon and went upstairs. I saw

Maggie and Mollie screaming at each other, pulling each other's hair out over something important like whether or not they were going to watch Nickelodeon or the Disney Channel. I didn't say a word. I just kissed them both on the forehead, told the *little shits* that I loved them more than anything in the world, and walked to the bedroom, where I climbed into bed, assumed a fetal position, and stayed for the rest of the night.

I can't say anything else on this subject, except of course, these three funerals did change me, and hopefully for the better.

AUNT JUTTA'S FAMOUS NOODLE KUEGEL

Preheat oven to 350 degrees

Butter a 9 x 13 Pyrex dish

12 Oz. egg noodles
¾ Stick margarine, melted
8 oz. Cream cheese
4 Eggs
½ Cup sugar
1 Small can crushed pineapple, drained
1 Small can apricot nectar

Cook the noodles, drain, and mix together all the ingredients.

¾ Stick of butter or margarine, melted
½ Cup of sugar
Cinnamon to taste
1 Cup crushed Corn Flakes

Mix together and crumble on top of the Kugel

Bake at 350 degrees for 55 minutes

(Some people, mainly adults, like to put a spoonful of sour cream on top. But that is optional.)

Chapter 17

Swappers Beware

Before Dick completely morphed into full-fledged "Psycho Dick," he and I actually were considered a pretty cute couple. This was, of course, decades ago, and the cuteness lasted only about 11 days (out of 14 years). But when we were cute, nothing could hold us back, except of course, my stupidity and naivete.

P.D., as I mentioned in earlier chapters, owned four restaurants with his brother in surrounding small towns. The two guys were kind of small-town celebrities which translated into, a) everyone who lived in this town had way too much free time on their hands and b) there was nothing better to focus on. They were both quite handsome, rugged guys, made pretty good money, and were well known for making the most delicious pizzas for miles around. Every morning they made their own homemade dough and homemade pizza sauce, and they used only the best mozzarella cheese. Together, the combination truly made an absolutely delicious pizza. When I first moved up to this godforsaken small town, I couldn't believe the line of customers wrapped around the restaurant waiting for it to open, night after night.

To be perfectly honest, looking back and knowing my sheer devotion to food, I'm not quite sure if it was the delicious pizza or my first orgasm (see Chapter 5) that made it impossible for me to say "no" when P.D. asked me to marry him after only 3 months of dating.

When we first got married, I sold my cute little green house in the "big city" and moved to a truly disgusting, dirty apartment above their largest restaurant. It always amazed me when I would come home to my gross apartment (we were newlyweds and had only been married for about 2 months) and see these strange, skinny women dressed in mini-skirts, flirting with my brother-in-law and P.D. They all had that Farrah Fawcett, bleached blonde shag thing going on (even though Charlie's Angels had been cancelled about 14 years before).

It hadn't taken long for me to notice that even though we were only about 3 hours away from the "big city," fashion, music, and fads were all about 10-15 years behind the times in this small town. These women were all radio advertising salespeople trying to sell "air time" for the restaurant. God forbid they try to sell on the "benefit/need" sales strategies implemented by Dale Carnegie. They all preferred to sell on sheer, disgusting flirtation.

As someone who tries to take my career choice seriously, sales people who do this (I've seen many men pull the same crap) make me absolutely crazy. It's kind of like how I feel when I meet someone who I know is Jewish and they tip less than 20 percent.Don't they all know what they are doing to my reputation?! (I'm sure they could not care less.)

Anyway, P.D. came home one afternoon and told me that we were invited to a dinner cruise on this old riverboat sailing along the Mississippi River. It was sponsored by the largest radio station in the city, and they wanted to thank all their largest advertisers. I was pretty excited. Not only was it the first time since our honeymoon that we went out, but it sounded like a lovely evening. I was starting to get a little lonely up there in South Bumblef*&@. I had never had a problem making friends before, but for some strange reason, I stuck out like a sore thumb in this town, and it took me a while to meet people.

I don't know if I ever mentioned this, but another thing Dick White did before we got married that totally made me think that I was marrying someone completely different was that, because he knew that I loved the water and adored the Lake of the Ozarks, he found and purchased this cute little $12,000 cabin (the outside deck was actually larger than the entire one-bedroom cabin) as a wedding present for me. It came with 1-1/2 acres of land right on the water and was located in the cutest, romantic cove you could imagine. (Unbelievable for only $12K!). We were both so excited with this purchase that we took his girls down there every weekend we could, and usually had a nice time. We bought a cheap boat, learned how to scuba dive, bought fishing equipment, painted and fixed up the cabin, and just did everything we could to pretend we were Ozark natives. (But I think our full set of teeth must have set us apart right away.)

We both got dressed up for the riverboat cruise. I was having one of those nights that you just feel pretty (they don't come very often, but when they do, you know it right away). We walked onto the boat, and I of course grabbed a delicious appetizer from one of the waiters, held P.D.'s hand while eating a rumaki and drank a Margarita at the same time (I am such a multitasker).

Within minutes, this young couple came up to Dick and me and introduced themselves to us. He was an optometrist who had several retail locations and his wife was a full-time aerobics class and tanning salon attendee. They seemed very nice and somewhat intelligent. She didn't look at me as if I were some sort of alien, like most women from South Bumblef*%@ did, so I liked her right away. They asked if they could have dinner at our table, and we said that would be wonderful.

P.D. and I were still in our "La La" phase of newlywed- and were pretty cozy. The strangest thing happened after dinner. As I was patiently waiting for dessert, because, three courses and six appetizers weren't quite enough for me, we all shared a bottle of wine, making "cute couples" small talk, when I realized that I had dropped my napkin.

As I bent down to grab my napkin from under the table, I saw that my new, leather-faced "BFF" had her hand on P.D.'s leg. She was rubbing him in this strange, almost manic, methodical motion. I'm not sure if P.D. was so drunk that he didn't know what was going on, or just really enjoying the sensation.

I think I went into a little bit of shock when I realized what the hell was going on. I found out later that this lovely couple were the town's most infamous "swingers." At this surreal moment in my life, here I am holding Dick's one hand while this spandex-wearing, skinny bitch is taking his other hand and guiding it toward her upper thigh.

As I was taking all this in, the "doctor" grabbed my hand, looked into my eyes, and said to me, very matter-of-factly, "Laura, I have to tell you something. Dick told me that you two are scuba divers." I just kind of blankly stared at him while his wife was grabbing my new husband's crotch and said, "Yes, we are." He said, "Well, I hope you know that I'm a diver, too!" I said, "Really? That's nice" (like I could really give a rat's ass at this moment!). He then said, "Yes, I'm a Certified Muff Diver."

I was so naïve, I did not know what the hell he was talking about. Still trying to be polite, I said, "Oh really? Did you get certified at the YMCA, too?" All of a sudden, he grabbed his wife's arm and said, "Come on, Honey. These two are way too stupid for us! Let's get the hell off this boat." I guess that sometimes ignorance pays off.

I couldn't for the life of me think of a recipe that went with this chapter, so I just thought a favorite saltwater fish dish would fit.

SVEN'S CRAB CAKES

Mix together the following:
16 oz. Crabmeat
2 Large eggs, beaten
5 Tablespoons of mayonnaise
1-1/3 Teaspoons of Old Bay seafood spice
1/3 Teaspoon of cayenne pepper
2/3 Cup of crushed crackers or breadcrumbs (I usually use Italian breadcrumbs)
1-1/3 Teaspoons chopped parsley
1-1/3 Teaspoons of yellow mustard

Mix all the ingredients together and cover. Refrigerate for about 2 hours before cooking.

Pan fry in hot oil and melted butter (in 50-50 combination) for 4-5 minutes (until a beautiful golden brown)

You can serve these alone with lemon wedges, or if you want, sometimes I make a béarnaise sauce (I use Knorr's packets, which you find with gravies and sauces at any grocery store.)

A gourmet tartar sauce also is delicious with them. I've always been a "Condiment Queen," so please don't mind me when I suggest how to make everything even more fattening with sauces.

Chapter 18

A Mensch Is A Mensch Is A Wonderful Smart-ass Mensch

(Warning: This chapter is not for the faint of heart, and should not be read by anyone under the age of 18; and by all means, it should never be read by my two daughters or anyone I know, because it's all pretty humiliating and nasty.)

You never forget the people who change your life. Many people have stuck through all my poor choices and loved me no matter what. But the one I talk about in this chapter is the attorney who took my case when I divorced P.D. for the second time.

No one would touch my case with a 10-foot pole. I remember when I went to one of the most well-known divorce attornies in the city. When she finally met with me, she was wearing this god-awful accordion skirt that made her tush look like it was as wide as my first car (a $300 Chevy Impala that I named "Old Blue"), and very thickly applied blue eye shadow from the bottom of her eyebrow down to her eyelid. I'm usually not mean, especially about butt sizes (I should never criticize anyone else's butt, trust me), but this woman was so mean to me during what was probably one of the most traumatic times of my life, that yes, I just wanted to be a bitch about her butt and outdated blue eye shadow. I promise, I would never do that to my friends like you!

She quickly skimmed through my 10-inch file of restraining orders, police reports, and degrading notes and tapes. You know, some people have keepsakes of jewelry and sweet photos; mine were all hours of tape recordings calling me a dumb whore and c*&% (probably the most insulting word in history; I can't even make myself spell it out!). We all need mementos along sweet "memory lane," don't you think?

When she finished going through all of the humiliating crap that had been my life for the last 14 years, she quietly said, in the most sympathetic voice she was able to muster, "You really have had a horrible time, haven't you? Don't worry Dear, I'll take your case." I sighed in huge relief for one millisecond, until she said "All I'll need is a $25,000 retainer." I was deeply touched — NOT!!! I actually think that she thought she was doing me a huge favor. A "woman helping another woman" kind of thing; someone who was put on the planet to help another human being when "rock bottom" had been reached. Again, NOT.

I had read that last year, her divorces included some governor who had cheated mercilessly on his wife, and a man who made millions on the discovery of a new and improved drywall. Unlike these two guys, I had a whopping $137 (give or take 39 cents) in my checking account that had to last the girls and me for the next month. I had a quick flash in my mind of the tellers at my bank, who knew how pathetic my financial situation was, laughing hysterically when someone from her office brought the $25,000 check into the bank to try to cash it. I may as well have tried to write it for $3 million.

I ended up leaving her office so damned humiliated that I wanted to wear a dark raincoat (even though it was 80 degrees and quite sunny that day) and huge black sunglasses. I realized that it was not going to be easy to get out of this horrible marriage for the second time while also protecting my kids from this man — who, after all, had told me that if I ever left him "the next time [I would] see my kids it would be on a milk carton,"

Anyway, a few days later, one of my co-workers at the phone company, who was aware of my depressing situation, told me to call her close friend. I'll describe the man who saved my life as a Jewish hippie lawyer who specializes in divorces for woman in dreadful circumstances. Benjamin has long, curly red hair (past his shoulders) and wire-rim glasses. He really would be a great character actor for some edgy FX or Lifetime for Women movie. Even though he has three kids and a lovely wife to support, he always loves helping "underdogs." He still works for many women's shelters and does a ton of pro bono work. He also helps many of the women whom he gets out of abusive marriages get back on their feet, finding them jobs. Many of them have been employed by him at his law office. Can you tell I love the guy and will never be able to thank him enough? He took my case without hesitation and without any retainer, and I am not exaggerating (this is, after all, a memoir, and I am always telling the truth, sordid as it can be), but through the entire ordeal, my total bill was about $900. I swore to myself, if and when I ever got out of this terrible situation, I would help women who were also in abusive situations as much as I possibly can. I've tried to do that, thanks to my role model and very dear friend.

The day of my divorce could not have come soon enough. The kids and I were in and out of hiding for months. I knew all the county police officers because they came over on a regular basis, making sure that P.D. didn't make good on any of his threats. I took a new job (the one I have now) that would hopefully pay me more so that I could take care of the three of us by myself because I knew that I would never end up getting any child support at all. Weeks before this great day, when I had a tinge of Jewish guilt, I decided to be as nice a soon-to-be ex-wife as possible, and told P.D. to take everything that he wanted out of the house (televisions, stereos, couches, whatever the hell he wanted — who cared about the "stuff"? I certainly didn't!).

The kids and I came back to the house the next day to find about 40 holes in the walls and as much destruction as a drunken P.O.S. could have achieved in 24 hours. It was pathetic. Here Maggie and Mollie were 2 and 4 years old, and this ass*%#@ destroyed their home. The next time I spoke with him, I asked him why on Earth he would destroy his children's home. And in his drunken, Dick Black type of voice, he answered, "*Because I f*&%$@% could!*" He always had a way with words.

My divorce day, June 20, 2000 (a day that I want to nominate as a national holiday) began with my mom, my sister Babs, my brother Johnny, and one of my best friends sitting with me in the courtroom. I was shaking like a leaf, I wasn't ready to humiliate myself in front of an entire courtroom. But, of course, I had to in order to make sure that I got full custody of the girls.

So here I was, sworn in and sitting in the witness chair, playing audio tapes to hundreds of complete strangers (who actually couldn't care less about my pathetic marriage, but probably found it quite entertaining while they were waiting for their turns. It was kind of like an X-rated, twisted, Arkansas version of Judge Judy, I guess). These people, whom I had never met, had to hear this man say things like "Okay, you whore, let me talk to my daughters so I can ask them how many d---- you sucked tonight." Or other loving comments such as, "Deep down, you f*&%$@*@ whore, you know that you really just want to f--- your brother Johnny." If someone could have told me that the girls and I could disappear forever and I would never have to see anyone who had heard the vile, horrendous things that the man that I trusted, loved, and married twice said to me, that would have been all right with me.

My reading audience probably is made up mostly of women, so I know you understand that, once you've given birth in a roomful of strangers, your sense of modesty disappears. Our humiliation quotient goes sky high. I also think, looking back on this horrific day, the experience (along with too many that I lived through with him) has instilled in me not just humility but also a mechanism that will never, ever allow me to take for granted Sven, my life now, my kids, my friends, and of course my attorney, Benjamin.

But I digress. After about an hour and a half of this crap, we were done. Sound the trumpets, blow the horns, thank God! It had seemed like forever. My mom, sister, brother, and friend left the courtroom and waited nervously to hear the verdict. P.D., of course, wanted me to pay alimony to him (can you believe it?). He wanted sole custody of the kids, and I don't know what the hell else (I think he put in his demands that I make him baklava every other Tuesday, too).

While we were sitting and waiting, something just came over me. After months of trying to keep it all together, I just all of a sudden lost it. I fell apart and started crying hysterically. I don't know if it was nerves, fear of the outcome, or just some kind of post traumatic shock. Whatever the hell it was, I was probably the biggest basket case I had ever been.

Finally, Benjamin walked through the courtroom doors, took my hand, and said, "Okay, Laura, we need to talk." I was shaking so badly that I was surprised that I could walk to the other side of the hallway with him. Thank goodness he had my arm. He looked at me and said, "OK, IT'S OVER. YOU'RE DIVORCED AND YOU HAVE THE KIDS."

I was so excited, I didn't know whether to scream, cry, or hug him profusely. I think I actually did all three. After a few minutes of my manic hysteria, he pulled me off him, looked me straight in the eye, and said, slowly and succinctly "I just want to tell you one thing, Laura. " I looked at him and asked quietly, "What, Benjamin? Tell me anything." And he said, "You marry him *AGAIN* and I'll f&*%ing KILL YOU!"

All of a sudden, my mother, brother, sister, and I think about 255 other people in the hallway, just cracked up and started laughing hysterically.

I think I laughed and cried uncontrollably for about 20 minutes.

For this chapter's recipe, I just wanted something that had "twice" in the recipe; and honestly, I've made these so often, I could make them in my sleep.

LOU'S TWICE-BAKED EASY CHEESY POTATOES

6 Large Russett Potatoes
¾ Stick of salted butter, softened
3/4 Cup of milk
½ Teaspoon of salt (optional)
6 Slices of American cheese
1 Package of shredded Colby cheese
(Bacon pieces and scallions – optional)

Wash potatoes and poke several holes with sharp fork in each . If you're in a hurry and don't have time to bake them in a conventional oven, just put potatoes on a microwaveable plate and bake on High for 20 minutes.

Check on them and, if necessary, re-arrange the potatoes on the plate and bake for another 10 minutes. Continue to cook 2 minutes at a time until they are done.

Let them cool for about 5 minutes (or use a towel to hold them so that you don't burn yourself).

Slice lengthwise. Scoop out the potatoes and put in the large bowl of an electric mixer. Add butter, milk and salt to taste. The trick is to beat on Medium for at least 5 minutes.

If the potatoes aren't creamy enough, add a little more milk to make the consistency of very creamy mashed potatoes.

In 9 x 13 Pyrex dish, scoop heaping spoons of potato in each shell, top with half slice of American cheese and
then heavily sprinkle with shredded Colby cheese.

Cover with aluminum foil and bake at 350 degrees for about 20 minutes right before you serve your meal.

Chapter 19

I Just Wrote A New Reggae Song In Honor Of Sven Called 'Youth Gone Bye-bye'

One day you finally realize that you are closer to the end of your life than you are to the beginning. You know, the realization that you will never learn how to "break dance," or wear a bikini again.

For me, it was the moment when, after Sven and I had finally gotten our hormonally charged, kicking and screaming daughters out the door for school, I quoted Paul Harvey. That was it. I was officially a middle-aged, middle-income American who is more interested in the commercials for overactive bladders and HoverRound scooters than the commercials for "the new and improved K-Y Jelly with fruity flavors."

Sven looked at me in bewilderment as he was writing on his "Rastafarian Wannabes R Us" blog, and said, "Don't even tell me, you have been listening to Paul Harvey?" I felt my face flush and thought, "Why the hell am I embarrassed by quoting words of wisdom from this sweet, wise octogenarian who had offered me so much wisdom and entertainment when I was stuck in "South Bumblef*&@" years ago, when I was married to P.D.. Then I thought, what the hell else was there to do when I was in S.B. with P.D.?

Paul (we're on a first name basis now) was talking about how not to raise children during this era, in which older, wealthier first-time parents want to give their children everything they didn't have growing up. Common sense snippets aimed towards parents and children like, "Don't ever give a brand new car to your 16-year-old" or, "I hope you get a black eye fighting for something you truly believe in." Another one I loved was, "I hope you have to share a bedroom with your brother or sister, and if they ever want to crawl under the covers with you because they are scared, let them in." Now, what the hell is so hokey about that? I thought it was sweet, and if I were a fan of that weird "stencil-on-the-wall, Amway cult-like fad," I would definitely be stenciling right now on my kids' walls.

Okay, I was going to stop writing about feeling old, but I guess I can just keep on going until I forget what I'm trying to explain (which by the way happens often) Don't you hate it when:

- You go to one of those dreaded high school reunions, and even though you really want everyone to realize how cute you turned out to be even though you couldn't get one damn date all through high school, everyone around you looks like they need to sign up for one of those scooters that you see advertised every 4-1/2 minutes on The Price is Right? You look at them and think, "Shit, I really am old. And God, I better increase the level of my bi-focals that I buy at the Dollar Store"

- You work with people that you know are your equals at work and then when they ask you to do their Numerology (see Chapter 5) when they are having problems with their love lives, and you realize they were born the year after you graduated college! (God, I hate that!)

- You can't even begin to get dressed without a pair of Spanx on. (That reminds me of my all-time favorite true story that my wonderful Aunt told me. She's going to kill me, but it's so damn cute, I have to share it with you)

My aunt — who was married for more than 40 years to a man she had known for only 2 weeks! (One of the best love stories of all time! Gives us romantics hope, doesn't it?) — told me that, after she tripped and fell and broke both her wrists, she needed her husband to help her put on her "control top" panty hose. While she lay on the bed, feeling just a wee bit humiliated, he sweetly, very carefully put them on.

She said, "Oh, thank you, Darling. I could not have done it without you." He then looked at her and said, just a little sheepishly,

"Honey, what would you like me to do with *the fat* that's hanging out?" With looks that I'm sure could have killed, my sweet aunt just looked at her dear husband and snarled, "Just tuck it in, Goddamit!" (I don't know why, but I just get tickled whenever I think of that story. Probably because I tuck it in myself every damn day!)

- You are out all night thinking that you are looking quite hot for an almost-50-year-old and then you get home, put your bifocals on to do the face washing/tooth brushing routine, and realize that you have a nose hair that is so long that anyone within a quarter mile of you can see it?

Okay, I'll stop now, but I'm going to warn you that I might come back to this chapter before I finish writing the book and add about 25 more.

The only recipe that I think would be appropriate for this chapter is something that is decadent and easy to make and that makes me forget that I am so damn old (but hotter than hell, nonetheless!)

NBF KIMMIE'S DECADENT CHOCOLATE CHEESECAKE BALL

8 oz. Cream cheese, softened
1 Stick of butter, softened
1/4 Teaspoon vanilla

Add 3/4 cup of confectioner's sugar
Add 2 Tablespoons of brown sugar

Mix well. Add 3/4 cup of mini chocolate chips. (I have used the semi-sweet and the milk chocolate chips here. You really can't go wrong ... it's all good!)

Chill at least 2 hours.

Form into ball. Chill at least 1 hour more.

Roll in chopped pecans (optional), and serve with assorted graham cracker sticks.

Chapter 20

What Do You Think About Quitting Our Day Jobs And Just Selling T-shirts That Will Change Our Lives?

I always think that I know myself very well. It may be just sheer cockiness or me living in a dream world. But, Laura Ray's self-awareness factor was quite high until I fell in love with my sweet, witty, talented, and quite the *smart ass* husband. He's always there to point out the obvious when I'm not seeing it in my own little *Laura Ray dream world*, hitting me over the head with a huge dose of reality (but in a nice way).

Anyway, Sven and I have become creatures of habit, and ever since he's settled in to my "suburban hell" at the house I had before we got married, he still has problems admitting to his friends, as well as to himself, that he actually lives in the 'burbs. Don't feel too sorry for him, he has kept his home in the city as a refuge, plus he always says that my home isn't near large enough for all of his albums.

We celebrate in our own little way once the kids have left the house and are on their way to school. We begin by breathing a heavy sigh of relief. Then Sven starts to make the coffee (perfect cup, every time!), and I turn on the television to MSNBC's Morning Joe. It's a fairly liberal, contemporary news program that we both enjoy, and it is great background noise while we do our "let's get ready for the real world" things.

One particular morning, a famous journalist was being interviewed by Joe and Mika, talking about the book he had just written. He was explaining how he got into the field of journalism, and how it all began when he saw a t-shirt when he was 15 years old that said,

"ALWAYS QUESTION AUTHORITY."

Well, yours truly had a huge " *aha moment*." I looked at Sven and said, "Oh my God, Honey, that is SO me!" Then I babbled, "If I could teach our kids anything at all, it's that. That is so damn profound. You know how much better the world would be, how many priests would not be able to get away with molesting children, how many wars would never ever begin, how many parents and teachers wouldn't abuse their children or students, and so forth, if everyone questioned authority?" Then I rambled on, "That is SO my motto and what I live by, and if everyone would just learn to just QUESTION AUTHORITY, what a better place this world would be!" Well, I was just going on and on about this, and I guess it was really amazing how animated I was, considering the fact that I hadn't had my coffee yet. Then, out of the corner of my eye, I saw Sven just look at me with *that face* and rolling his eyes. And then he said, "Oh, Honey, I love you so much, but you really are so full of shit!" I looked at him in astonishment and thought, "My God, how can this man, who I have slept with for 6 years now and love so deeply, not know how important this is to me and how this is really the center of all my beliefs? He then looked at me drolly and, in a monotone, (he hadn't had his coffee yet, either), he finished his thought by saying, "Honey, love of my life…" (he always says that right before he packs a wallop), "Your t-shirt shouldn't read "ALWAYS QUESTION AUTHORITY." Your t-shirt should read, "PLEASE BE MY FRIEND, AND WOULD YOU LIKE TO TRY MY MUSHROOM DIP?"

In that split second, as we both realized that he was so right, we just burst into such hysterical laughter that tears were running down our cheeks (and I was lucky that I had already peed.) I just looked at him and thought, "God, this man knows me so well, it's scary."

I then thought, "isn't it funny how we all see ourselves so totally differently than who and what we really are. That self-awareness factor that I mentioned at the beginning of this chapter totally went out the window.

So, please be my friend, and would you like to try this delicious mushroom dip?

LOLA'S DELICIOUS MUSHROOM DIP

Preheat oven to 350 degrees

In a nice Pyrex dish (one size smaller than 9 x 13), mix in the following:
1 Cup sour cream
1 Cup of Hellmann's mayonnaise
1 Cup of shredded cheddar cheese
2/3 Cup of shredded Parmesan cheese
16 oz. Stems/Pieces of mushrooms (any type you'd like)
1 Package of Good Seasons Mild Italian dry salad dressing mix

Stir together all of the above in the baking pan and bake for 45 minutes (or until golden brown).

Serve with Parmesan crostini or your favorite crackers. Enjoy!

Chapter 21

"Oh, Mommy, Why Are You So Darn Materialistic?"

I just want to begin this chapter by saying that although I'm not very proud of myself for writing this, I'd better 'fess up and admit to all of you that I, Laura Ray, am not perfect, not by a long shot. Just ask my children or my husband. But, I really wanted to write this chapter for every woman out there who is reading this who has been just a little disappointed after a birthday or especially a Mother's Day that has come and gone.

Sven always says that when I begin to talk about this subject, I always end up sounding clichéd, but I'll apologize right up front, because I know that you, my new best friends, my readers, will totally understand the point I'm trying to make. I'm hopeful, just as I am about "world peace," even though I really don't think men or children will ever "get it."

Okay, so I earn a nice income and have survived in an industry where I'm one of two left from a training class of 27. I'm so thankful that I even have a job that allowed me to take care of my children when I was a single mom with no child support. It's a high pressured commission based job where Sven ends up having to recruit close friends and family to take turns to help get me out of the *fetal* position lodged under my desk at the end of every month. I'm very thankful to those before me who fought and won for equal pay for equal work and the right to vote (duh!), along with all the basic rights to do what we feel necessary to our own bodies. But, as working mothers, we're all supposed to be good providers, gourmet cooks, child psychologists, good housekeepers (unless you can afford to hire one — which of course with two teenagers, I don't have that luxury), maintain a size 6 figure (or size 8, if the clothes run small), be great in bed, and be a creative Room Mother, a Girl Scout leader, and a swim team timer all at the same time.

I won't stereotype men. I wouldn't do that, even though I think it would be a safe call if I did. Most men are pretty much "done" for the day when they get home from a hard day at the office, and they don't mind at all that their small gut is protruding over their belt buckle. All these negative thoughts (which I just don't have the time to go to a psychologist to get off my chest because I'm too frigging busy taking care of everyone else) just brings me back to Mother's Day. Do you now see where I'm going with this? I know you do, because you all "*get it*"!

Okay, so even though I know in the back of my mind that Sven and my two lovely daughters had not hired a marching band to play the theme song from Doctor Zhivago (for those who don't know, it's called Lara's Theme — different spelling, but hell, it's beautiful and I'll take it for my theme song) or hired a pilot to sky write, "WE LOVE YOU MOM, AND BY THE WAY, THANKS FOR BEING THE BEST MOMMY IN THE WORLD" (I know that would cost a small fortune, and knowing that that we had only $128 in our checking account on that sad Sunday, that was probably out of the question). And yes, I know that Sven is not the biological father of our two lovely high maintenance daughters (even though he has been their daddy for over half of their lives and is really the only father they've ever known).

But, that still doesn't seem to matter when your mind wanders to the many times in the last 3 months where, for instance, I'm carrying a homemade chocolate chip pancake on my lap with a glass of milk spilling in my car while driving the kids to school still wearing my pajamas after they missed the bus (for the third time that week) and I'm trying to make sure that they eat a warm breakfast, or that no one in the entire frigging family will even begin to think about what's for dinner or, God forbid, set the table until I get home from a day of being screamed at by 23 customers. Or maybe, when I'm driving a kid to the 24-hour grocery store at 11:55 PM to buy white chocolate and Oreo cookies so that she can make a birthday cake "Oreo Ball" in the shape of her best friend Hanna's head. Or maybe just going into $20,000 worth of debt trying to pay for our youngest kid's Bat Mitzvah (it was beautiful by the way, and she did a fantastic job!), or have an entire third-grade class (that would be three classes of 22 8- and 9-year-olds) over to our home because Mollie decided it would be nice to have a wedding shower for her favorite teacher (at the time), or make a grilled turkey, cheese and bacon sandwich for a kid who refused to eat anything all day because she hadn't decided whether or not she wanted to be anorexic (something she had seen on an episode of "Daily Affliction", or "Celebrity Addiction" or some other *effing* (pardon my language — can you tell this subject totally enrages me?) horrible reality-based television show on TLC (all of which, let me say, popped up after that damn writers' strike). And then decided that no, she didn't like that feeling of "hungry" and so she woke me up at 2 AM so that I could make her favorite sandwich, or cook an elegant, gourmet dinner (beef tenderloin with both a Bernaise and a Peppercorn sauce) for my husband's favorite band when they happened to be in our city (but because he wasn't flying home from Jamaica until that night, had to do it all myself), or buy and hand out 500 cupcakes on a major urban street to celebrate "National Record Store Day" after working her ass off at a job that is primarily a commissions job who's company's commission system broke, so never really knows if she's going to paid or not, or wash and sanitize about 438 sheets and towels when our kid had swine flu and puked all over the house while I was running her to the emergency room freaking out over a 106-degree temperature.

Yes, I know I'm rambling and getting a little hysterical about this subject. And I know that I'm not telling you anything new about what we mothers do every damn day of our lives. But, one day a year, one damn day should be the day that families hire skywriters, who risk their lives to thank us, and maybe the Messiah could have the time to stop everything and say, "Gee, thanks to all of those moms for being so fabulous." Is that too much to ask? I know I'm being dramatic, but I haven't touched on even a percentage of the stuff we all do every damn day.

While I was folding the sixth batch of laundry on Mother's Day, almost all of it the girls' clothes, while I could hear them beating the crap out of each other with their new iPods (I kid you not), I started to cry. My older, more hormonal one, came up to me and said, "Why are you crying, Mom?"(as if she didn't know that her grabbing a clump of hair out of her sister's head wouldn't upset me), and I said, "Well, if you're not going to get me a damn present for Mother's Day, the least you could do is to be nice to each other for one single day." Tears were flowing down my cheek, and I wasn't quite into my ugly cry, but very close. And then she looked at me and said, "So, you're crying because we didn't buy you a present, aren't you?" And then she answered her own question saying, "God Mom, why do you have to be so darn materialistic?"

Simple to make, absolutely delicious and addicting (and a show stopper) if you want to bring them to a party— whether or not you make them in the shape of Hanna's head.

AUNT ETHEL'S OREO BALLS

8 oz Cream cheese, softened
1 Full package of Oreo cookies
1 Package of white chocolate bark, (Ghirardelli white chocolate chips also work well)
Dark chocolate bark (or Ghirardelli semisweet chocolate chips)

In the work bowl of a food processor, crumb the Oreo cookies. Mix in the softened cream cheese and refrigerate for about 30 minutes.

Roll the cookie mixture into small balls and dip each ball into the melted white chocolate to completely cover. If you'd like, you can then drizzle the dark chocolate mixture over the white chocolate to give it a professional effect. After each ball has been dipped, place it on a cookie sheet.

Refrigerate to let the chocolate cool before serving.

Chapter 22

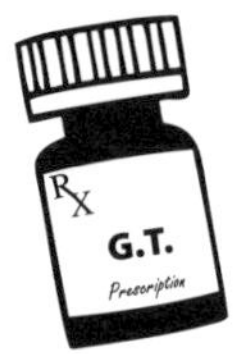

You'll See TV Commercials About This New Disease Soon

I have to admit that I, Laura Ray have a horrible disease. You may never have heard of it before; in fact, I think I may have just made it up. But, let me tell you, this disease can be debilitating. It can destroy families and friendships and leave one in financial ruin. This disease is contagious. It affects the completely innocent and unsuspecting. It can also be passed down from generation to generation and will probably make it into the New England Journal of Medicine once my book is printed in its ninth edition.

This disease is called "Generosity Tourrettes" (I'll call it G.T. for short). There will probably be G.T. Anonymous groups (and a parent group of G.T. Family Members) sprouting up all over the country, and perhaps all around the world, very soon. Once you read this, you will probably realize that you've had this disease for years, and never even knew you had it or that you are a carrier of the gene.

Please let me explain. Hopefully, you have not been afflicted by this horrible condition. The symptoms are simple: Words come vomiting out of your mouth, and you have no control whatsoever when they start spewing. Stupid, horrible words that you regret the instant that they leave your mouth, such as

"Don't worry, I'll make the 20 briskets for the funeral. When would you like them delivered?"

"If you need a place to live for a while, we have a nice mother-in-law's quarters down in our basement. I'm sure that Sven won't mind!"

"I know you are totally broke. Don't worry— I get paid next Friday. I'll give you half of my paycheck; I'm sure it won't throw a wrench into our everyday expenses."

"Oh, you're going to have surgery next week? I'll make sure that your family has nice meals for the next month while you recuperate."

"So, you need volunteers for face painting 500 children for 10 hours in 98-degree heat? That's all right; I'll bring my entire family to do it next Saturday. Would it be possible for you to first teach us all how to paint?"

"That's so romantic that you and Brad want to get married but you can't afford it. Don't worry! You can have it at our home. I've never given a wedding reception, but I'm sure I could put it together all by myself, and I promise it will be beautiful!"

"You need a deejay for your daughter's thirtieth birthday Saturday night and can't find one in your price range? No worries! My husband would love to do it, and of course he won't charge you."

"I know that I just met you here at the gas station, but you seem so sweet, and if you don't have a place to live, my husband has a very nice home in the city that I'm sure he wouldn't mind you living in for a few weeks for free until you get your life back in order."

"I'm sure it would be all right with my family if your daughter used our basement to detox. We'll be upstairs just in case she needs our help."

"You can't afford a lawyer? Let me call my brother and see if he can look at your case; he won't charge you. He's not a 'typical lawyer'; he's a really, really nice one!"

I have just one thing to say (and yes, I did indeed say and do each of these horrible, yet well-meaning things, which really did all come from my heart). The sad thing is that, after these things have already spewed, you get this really sick feeling in the pit of your stomach, and you then immediately think...

WHAT THE F&%@ WAS I THINKING?!

Who the hell do I think I am? Who gave me the right to volunteer other people's time, money, and services just because

I get this bug up my butt to try and do the right thing and make myself feel better for some, who knows, really bad thing I did in a past life when I was a rat or a dog or a really mean pirate? (I'm thinking Buddhist at the moment.)

Then I make myself feel even more guilty, thinking, "How often have I spent our kids' inheritance, my husband's and my early retirement (that's a joke!), and, most important, countless hours of valuable and impossible-to-find 'free time' that I could be spending alone with Sven and/or the kids instead of on all these dumbass ideas?" Although, they are always appreciated, and people will always end up thinking kind thoughts about you (even though, in the back of their minds, they really are thinking, "What a schmuck!") But then, through absolutely no fault of their own, they will get the residual effects of the disease, and then they start to spew words from their mouths, such as:

> *"You've been so nice, you wouldn't mind if I used your extra vehicle for a week while mine is in the shop, would you?"*
>
> *"You've helped us so much, would you mind if I used your credit card for a week while we get our finances in order? I'll pay you back the second I get paid!"*
>
> *"Thanks so much for letting us stay at your home. You wouldn't mind if we left our 104-pound, almost-housebroken Russian wolfhound at your home while we go on an emergency vacation at the beach? I'm sure his epileptic seizures won't flare up again!"*

So, as I was doing my own research on this terrible disease and before I submit it to the American Medical Association, I thought I would help the medical researchers out and give them a few things that I have already come up with.

First of all, I'm sure that the cure for this ailment, besides many years of therapy, will be some kind of Prozac-type of drug. The amount prescribed will be based upon the number of times "G.T. spewing" occurs. If spewing occurs more than once in a 24-hour period, then the full dose is required. If it occurs only once or twice a month, you would probably be able to cut the dose in half. The drug-induced therapy will help to curb the *chutzpah* to offer yours and other unsuspecting people's services, money, and time without thinking how it will affect everyone.

(For the two readers out there who don't know what *chutzpah* means, I'll give you the definition that my Dad always loved to use: "The boy who kills his mother and father and then pleads for mercy from the court because he's an orphan." Boy, that's an old one!)

I am also sad to say that my in-depth scientific studies on G.T. have shown that it is passed down from generation to generation. Through my extensive research, I've come to the conclusion that there is a 9 percent probability that it can be passed down from mother to son, a 0.2 percent probability that it will be passed down from father to son (let's face it, most guys don't get this at all!), and most important, a 98.3 percent chance that it's passed down from mother to daughter, who will never know what has hit her.

Just last week I got a phone call from the father of my daughter's best friend telling me that it was so nice of Mollie to have offered our home and swimming pool for a surprise birthday party/BBQ for his wife. He had totally forgotten that it was his wife's birthday and was gone all weekend on a motocross weekend with his buddies. It wasn't a huge birthday, but a birthday nonetheless, and because he needed to get out of the "doghouse" that he had put himself into, he wanted to make sure that my daughter's offer was all right with me.

I just looked at the phone for several moments, sadly realized that I couldn't be angry with my sweet daughter for spewing, and quietly told the guy that the party could start at 7 PM. It's not her fault that those horrible words spewed. It's all part of the disease, and she got a really bad case of it from her mother.

I thought I should have a recipe that can be made for a lot of people at a moment's notice:

AUNT BOO'S STRAWBERRY PECAN PRALINE SALAD

1 Large bag of pre-washed, ready-to-serve Romaine lettuce
1 Small Bag of pre-washed, ready-to-serve Spring Mix
1 pint of large strawberries
2 Cups of Hoody's Praline Pecans (if you can't find these in the produce section at your grocery store, look for other candied pecans, usually in the baking aisle)
1 pint of washed and sliced mushrooms
2 Chopped Scallions
1 Bottle of Poppyseed Salad Dressing (Aunt Boo prefers Marzetti's which you can find refrigerated in the produce section)
1 Cup of Croutons

In large, pretty salad bowl, toss the Romaine, Spring Mix, mushrooms and scallions together. Then generously place sliced strawberries, pecans, and croutons on top of the salad. Present like that, and right before you serve it, toss with the refrigerated poppyseed salad dressing (to taste).

People will go nuts (Get it? See? Nuts over the nuts?)

Chapter 23

Southern Hospitality Brought To A Whole New Level

I'm actually writing this chapter as something like a "Laura Ray Public Service Announcement." With all the horrible things going on right now with corporate "pigdom," including all the banking scandals, political crap, and oil spills resulting from corporate greed that will take generations to fix, I'm sure you feel the same way I do. I can't even watch the news without crying and puking about the things that people whom we have no control over are doing to this beautiful world that God gave us, all for the almighty buck.

So, if you're like me, you just trudge along every day doing your very best with your daily 8 AM to 8 PM job, trying to avoid those horrible, shocking pink disconnect notices, making sure you have enough money left over to spoil your children, and then do your best to attend to the social needs that we, as *women of the millennium*, have got into our brains that it is our responsibility to address in our free time.

So, this is the point where I will tell you how someone, a total stranger thousands of miles away from me, totally restored my faith in human nature. This one sweet, unsuspecting woman, who has no idea that she's going to be in my book (I hope she's not upset with me when she finds out), truly did a deed that changed my whole viewpoint of humanity.

I'll start at the beginning. Last week was a horribly tumultuous week for the Ray household. Actually, the rest of the immediate family was unscathed; it was me who was in the middle of a total breakdown. It came at the tail-end of helping to throw a wedding reception for a dear friend of mine, a reception that she couldn't afford to host (that damn G.T. again). Two days later, one of our family's dearest friends passed away at the disgustingly young age of 46 after fighting a long and hard fight against leukemia. She had gone through a perfect bone marrow transplant, was told that she was in remission, and then, when she went to the doctor for her monthly checkup, found out that it had come back with a vengeance. They gave her just 3 weeks to live. This gorgeous woman was a mother of four kids, and just typing this makes me cry, so I'll stop. Anyway, my entire family (who are all terribly afflicted with G.T.) were involved in hosting, cooking and cleaning for 100 of this woman's closest friends.

In the midst of all of this, my fabulous sister-in-law in Jacksonville, Florida, was having bypass surgery. With the wedding I was hosting, the funeral crap, and my very high-pressure job (I'm leaving out swim meets, Girl Scout meetings, yada yada yada...you get the point), I couldn't think of a way I could actually fly down to Florida to help out.

I did the next best thing I could think of at the time: I got on the phone and started to lecture every person who was living with this saintly woman. I can be so pushy sometimes; but my brother-in-law, cousins, and other sister-in-law swore to me that they would care for my sister-in-law in the same manner that I would. I don't know if I was just desperate to believe that they would, but I was relieved, and my guilt level was lowered a few notches. I just knew that these middle-aged, intelligent people were quite capable of taking care of and properly feeding someone who just had major surgery. Right? Shouldn't be over the realm of probability, right? NOT!

Have you ever heard the saying, "When it rains, it pours"? Well, as I was driving downtown to help with the funeral, I got a call from the woman who has been my best friend since I was 10 years old, who told me that she had been trying to reach me for days to tell me that her 17-year-old son had been hospitalized. Apparently, he had a virus that made him cough so badly that he had blown a hole in his lungs, and air pockets escaped into his body and could have killed him. (Is it just me, or is that one of the strangest things you've ever heard? I've never heard of that before, even with Maggie being the "Queen of Mysterious Diagnoses.") Anyway, she sounded horrible and was in "hospital Hell." I told her to not worry, that after I did my thing at the funeral, I would run back to the county and bring her and her son their favorite Japanese chicken bowls. What the hell was I thinking? You know, with all my free time in between work and everything else...what a joke!

The only time I ever have to make the phone calls I need to make all day is, of course, in the car (very carefully, may I add and I NEVER text). On the way to the hospital to drop off the chicken bowls, I called my sister-in-law to check up on her. She sounded horrible. I said, "Are you okay?" She said, very quietly in her sweet southern drawl, "Oh, I'm just fine." I replied, "Well, you don't sound fine. You actually sound horrible! Where is everyone? Are they at the house taking care of you?" She said, "No, they all had to leave, I'm here by myself."

Well, my face was flushed, and if I had screamed as loudly as I wanted to, she would have had to go back to the hospital for a cochlear implant. I said, "Why the hell would they have left you all alone just days after surgery? They promised me that they wouldn't leave you alone!" She said, "Don't worry, Honey, I'm just fine."

The one question that always pops into my mind is of course about food, so I asked, "What did they make you for dinner before they left?" She said, "Oh, well...I just got myself up and made me a delicious peanut butter and jelly sandwich." Well, with that you could have just stabbed me in the heart and I wouldn't have felt a thing. I couldn't believe that she had to make her own meal (if you can call peanut butter and jelly a meal). I was so angry and felt so frigging guilty at the same time. If I could have possibly flown down that very second and beaten the crap out of the family I love, I would have.

This really should not have been such a cataclysmic, end-of-the-world thing like I'm making it out to be. I guess that with the funeral, the end-of-the-month sales stress, the wedding, and the blown lung, the peanut butter and jelly sandwich was just the thing that pushed me over the edge.

When I got to the hospital, I set up lunch for my friend and her son. I then went out to the hospital corridor (where the phone reception is absolutely horrendous), and called the Olive Garden, one of my sister-in-law's favorite restaurants.

A very nice hostess got on the phone, and I proceeded to tell her that I needed to order one of everything on their "Heart Healthy" menu. She said, "My, that's a lot of food. Are you sure you want to order *everything*?" I was thinking that, not only would this alleviate my terrible guilt for not being there, but most importantly. it would ensure that my sweet sister-in-law, as well as the entire family, would have enough healthy food for the next week or two. (It wouldn't be as healthy or delicious as my matzoh ball soup, but it was as good as it was going to get for now!)

It took about 15 minutes to decide the ratio of Pasta Fagioli soups to salad and breadsticks we would need; but afterwards, once the heavy math was over, I started to give her my credit card.

She abruptly stopped me in her slow southern drawl and said, "I'm sorry, Honey, but we can't take credit cards over the phone." I stopped and, a little shocked, said, "Well, pardon my French, but how the hell am I supposed to pay for all this food that you're going to deliver when I'm in St. Louis and you are in Jacksonville?" And then I started to go into my pleading mode (that's the mode right before I start losing it and crying), and she said, "Ma'am, it's a corporate policy, and I just can't take any credit cards over the phone." The pleading mode in high gear, I said, "I will give you my secret whammy secure ID code, my blood type, my phone numbers, my mother's maiden name, my 15-pound Chihuahua, anything you want…if you just take this damn credit card." She very firmly said, "I'm sorry, but the answer is NO." Well, I then went from sweet to pissy and said, "I want to talk to your manager *right* now!"

She handed the phone to her manager.

"Hellooooo, this is Arlene, the District Manager here at Olive Garden. May I help you?"

By then, I was practically in tears, and started to explain to this complete stranger the week from hell I was having, and that she could be a huge part of making it so much better if she would just make one damn exception and take my gosh darn credit card…just this once. She sweetly and softly said, "I'm really sorry, Ma'am, that you've had such a bad day, but I just absolutely cannot take your credit card over the phone. It's company policy, and I just can't break the rules."

I could feel myself starting to hyperventilate and all of the blood rush to my head, when she said in an almost angelic voice, "Well, I have an idea. How about if I just 'comp' your entire order and then when you happen to come down to Jacksonville to visit one day, you can just write us a check for the amount!"

I stared at the phone and paused for about 11 minutes in a state of semi-shock and asked, "So, let me get this right. You won't take my credit card over the phone to pay for this huge bill, but you'll give the whole thing to me for free, trusting that I will pay you back if and when I come to Jacksonville? Is that what you're saying?"

She said, again in that sweet voice, "Exactly."

I hope that everyone who ever stops by that Olive Garden located on the north side of Duvall County will tell this wonderful woman that not only did she restore my complete faith in humanity, but that her strange, but very sweet gesture helped to bring my sister-in-law back to perfect health!

This is a delicious, award-winning recipe that you won't need a credit card for.

ITALIAN EGGPLANT A LA LOU SUE

Preheat oven to 350 degrees

1 Large Eggplant sliced lengthwise
1 Cup of sliced and washed mushrooms
¾ Cup of chopped onion
1 Cup of Italian breadcrumbs
½ Stick Butter
1 Cup of tomato sauce (I prefer Prego)
1 tsp. of minced garlic
1 Tablespoon of chopped parsley
Salt and pepper to taste
1 Cup of Shredded Mozarella Cheese
1 Cup of Shredded Mild Cheddar Cheese

Score around the two eggplant halves and then scoop out the meat of the eggplant, cutting into small chunks.

In sauté pan, melt butter and sauté eggplant chunks, mushrooms, onions, garlic, for 3 to 5 minutes.

Stir in Italian bread crumbs and add salt and pepper.

Place the eggplant halves in a 9 x 13 Pyrex dish.

Spread ½ Cup of tomato sauce into each eggplant half.

Then evenly spoon in ½ of the eggplant mixture into each eggplant half.
Sprinkle ½ Cup of Mozarrella and ½ Cup of Mild Cheddar cheese on each eggplant half.

Top with chopped parsley (approximately ½ tablespoon on each eggplant half.

Bake for 30 to 40 minutes until golden brown.

Chapter 24

Any Way You Slice It, Dating After 40 Sucks

None of us ever thought that we'd be single at this stage in our lives. When you were walking down the aisle all starry eyed and beautiful, didn't you think that you would be with the man you loved until you were both about 100 years old and ready to leave this world, holding hands as you enter into eternity together?

Well, maybe I'm exaggerating just a little, or I've read way too many love stories. But after living with a verbally abusive, often cruel man for give or take 14 years, after the divorce I realized that I am a person who loves marriage but just viscerally hated her husband.

Maybe it's because I'm a five (see Chapter 5), but reality hit me when one of my best friends walked into our home soon after the divorce (and right after I finished fixing the 40 holes in the drywall that P.D. had punched in) and said, "Lou, why the hell do you still have pictures of P.D. in your house?" I looked at her as if she had lost her mind, and then I suddenly realized what she was talking about.

As I was looking at the framed photo in the living room I quietly replied, "*That's not P.D., that's my father*!" It struck me then that I could have been a poster child for *Children of Alcoholics Who Become Enabling Co-Dependents*.

Only then did I know that I needed to finally break the horrible cycle of abuse. God forbid that my two beautiful little girls would do what I did and marry someone who looks like and treats them just like their father. *Please, just kill me now*!

So that is why, when I finally was single again at age 40, I was bound and determined to find a wonderful man so that Maggie and Mollie could see what a truly loving relationship was really like. Even though, I didn't have a clue in hell on how to do it because let's face it, I didn't know what to do when I was in my 20s. If we all wrote about our horrible dating experiences in our 20s, 30s, 40s and beyond, this book would be longer than War and Peace.

Well, since I knew my taste in men totally sucked, I decided to let others pick out men for me to date. I decided to go to a very well-known and quite expensive "lunch dating service." Not bad; combining food with meeting the love of your life should be a good thing, right? NOT!

The service, if it had worked like it was supposed to, was going to cost me $800. This ended up being about $100 per date. (By the way, I actually have 6 dates left on the service if anyone out there would like to give it the old "college try." (I'm not sure if they are transferable; I never did read that damn fine print.)

Anyway, thinking that the woman who sold me the service truly cared about my love life, I poured my heart and soul out to her. I told her that the most important things in my life were my children, family and friends. I told her that my last 14 years were basically hell and I really wanted to show my kids what love was all about, yadda, yadda, yadda.

Well, she methodically wrote it all down and nodded her head at all my babbling as if she understood and really cared about me. She had me sign the contract and then fixed me up with my first date. I was so excited that she had found "the one" so quickly. I thought, "Hell, this dating stuff is easy, what the heck is everyone bitching about?" The guy was a pilot who had never been married, never been in a long term relationship, and didn't really like kids at all. (He said that he had seen so many obnoxious children on airplanes, it killed any paternal longing he ever had. I would go out on a limb and say that this guy had never had any paternal longings, ever - in his entire body.) What killed me most was when he told me that he hated his entire family; he called them "trailer trash." At that point, all I could say was, "Check. please!"

The second date was with a very nice looking, artsy-fartsy architect with long hair and a very "old hippie" vibe to him. I quickly dismissed all the bad feelings I had for the dating service and for the horrible match with the pilot. My first thought was, "This man is wonderful. I'm so glad that I took this leap of faith, expensive as it was." That was, of course, until he told me during coffee after lunch that he had to tell me the truth: he had a 24-year-old son living with him, who probably always will live with him and who was diagnosed with sociopathic schizophrenia and refuses to take his meds. "Check, please!"

Needless to say, I decided that I would take my losses and just try dating on my own. Screw the dating service. I couldn't do any worse, could I?

I also had many friends who wanted to fix me up with their cousins, brothers, bosses, etc. It was very sweet of them, but it ends up being terribly awkward when it doesn't work out.

It was then that I decided to let my friend (the one who thought my father was P.D.) sign me up with an on-line Jewish dating service. She decided that my bad luck with men was not due to my choosing an abusive, P.O.S. alcoholic; it was the fact that he wasn't Jewish! I was to the point of trying anything, and I figured, at least he won't be an anti-Semite like P.D.

The first guy who I met through this service (we'll call him "Ted") was a middle-aged, semi-handsome guy who had one son and worked for a major designer shoe wholesaler. He travelled all over the world, especially to Italy, buying shoes to sell in the U.S. Even though I'm not a shoe fanatic and I love D.S.W. more than the expensive designer brands, I thought he sounded promising. He had a job, a kid who wasn't heavily medicated; hell, I was on a roll.

We met at a nice restaurant for a drink and then for dinner. I noticed that talking to Ted was like pulling teeth. I always thought that I was pretty easy to talk to and a fairly good conversationalist, but I swear, trying to talk with this guy was murder! I finally decided that, if all else fails, let's talk "current events."

I mentioned how fantastic it was that the medical researchers had found a possible way to cure Parkinson's and Multiple Sclerosis through use of stem cells. He didn't even bat an eye or budge when, almost in tears, I talked about how one of my best friends in the world has had M.S. since she was 24 and how this research is giving her, along with millions of others, hope that there is a cure to these horrible diseases in the very near future. He looked at me and — I swear to God — he said in a total monotone, "I really don't have time for shit like that. I have shoes to sell."

"Check, please!"

I then met a Jewish psychiatrist (aka: The Kiss of Death. We'll call him "Elliott") who I (unfortunately) dated on and off for over a year.

I finally started to feel pretty darn good about myself until of course, I met him. I've come to the conclusion that most psychiatrists are just friggin nuts! (And I apologize if I'm offending someone out there, but that's what I truly think)

He'd always get upset with me, telling me that I was being "passive aggressive" or "narcissistic." It got to the point that I really wanted to ask him to just start speaking English, and if he wanted to degrade me, just use the simple terms that I was called every day by P.D., like "f*&$ed up bitch" or "shit for brains" or worse. He also had a strange tendency to "retreat" every 3 weeks or so. He would "hole up" for about five days wearing this nasty bathrobe in his disgustingly dirty two-bedroom home (where I'll bet you $100, if you walked in today — which is about 10 years later — he would still have this one dusty Tylenol on the floor right by the bathroom door. It was kind of a game I played with myself to see how long it would take for him or his kids to pick it up).

My favorite story about Elliott was when his son was Bar Mitzvah'd. Prior to the big Bar Mitzvah, he would break up with me every few months, telling me that he couldn't trust me, or my passive-aggressive tendencies bothered him too much. Then, a few weeks later, he would let me know he couldn't live without me — until, of course, the time came that he had to retreat for another week in his hole. (Do you understand any of this crap? If you do, you're a lot more intelligent than I was, because it was way over my head!)

Well, he definitely didn't want to live without me during the Bar Mitzvah. Basically, that was because he needed my help with doing numerous things. I was in charge of buying and putting together lovely baskets for the "out of towners," baking goodies for 150 people and a few other chores that I've repressed (due to the fact that I feel like a schmuck every time I think of how much time and money I spent on him).

His family came into town for the big event. They were all these very New York, upper-class people, the kind where all the women were these little, teeny tiny Jewish women who all wore size "negative two" clothing. Elliott begged me not to tell his family that I had married and divorced P.D. twice. He said he was very embarrassed by that little fact. He made me feel like he was finally bestowing the honor of allowing me to meet his family. His Uncle Lefty looked at me and said, "Why, you must be one of those 'Farmer Jews' that they grow big in the Midwest?" I had no idea how to reply to that comment.

After a very long weekend with these people (it was only two and a half days, but it seemed like an eternity), I crawled back home and into my bed feeling like a total loser, wondering why I put up with people treating me so horribly? Maggie, who was about 7 then, sensed my despair and crawled into my bed and said, "Mommy, you look really, really sad. If you love me, you won't date Elliott anymore, O.K.?" That's all it took. I was completely finished with that relationship. All I can say is that sometimes it just takes the wisdom of a 7-year-old to get your head out of your rear and to start thinking clearly again!

So, I decided that most men our age must look into different mirrors than we do. They must see themselves as someone totally different than what they really are, because most of them that I met think they deserve a woman who earns $150,000 per year woman and looks like Pamela Anderson. Oh well, I wish every damn one of them good luck! By the way, I went on the same dating website a few months ago to find a date for my aunt, and when I plugged in my age range just for shits and grins, I found the same group of men who were there when I first started dating. The funny thing is they still have their same pictures on the site. Aren't they lucky that they haven't changed at all in 10 years?

I'm really writing this all as another "Public Service Announcement" to make all of you single women out there feel a little better about your dating life after reading all of my pathetic tales.

The last guy that I want to tell you about was probably the most handsome guy I had ever dated (except for Sven, of course). I'll call him "Timothy," and I didn't actually meet him — Maggie and Mollie did. He owned a landscape company that did some work for the neighbors across the street. He was so sweet, as his staff was doing all the hard work, he was teaching the girls how to plant flowers and eating Happy Meals with them. He was so charming, I would look out the window at them and just melt. Supposedly, Mollie looked at him one day and said, "Timothy, will you marry our mommy?" He looked at her and said, "Well I don't know, Honey. Maybe I should date her once before I marry her?" We dated for a few months. He was kind and very generous. The kids were in "la la land" until, of course, he called to tell me that he was in jail for his third DUI and he needed me to give him $3,000 to get him out on bail. Don't you just hate when that happens? After reading my chapter on G.T., I'll let you decide whether or not I gave him the money he needed.

I really don't regret any of my horrible dates. I know that they all were for one reason: the cosmic purpose of loving and fully appreciating Sven. I would not have ever met him had I not put myself "out there" in the land of "Dating Hell." Well, maybe the next volume of this book should be called "Still Brain Dead and Cooking" and I can start the chapters with some of your stories.

I thought this great recipe (which I've made often) was a perfect fit for this chapter. It basically kills two birds with one stone without even trying.

S.O.S. GODIVA CHOCOLATE MARTINI

1-1/2 shots Godiva Chocolate Liqueur
1-1/2 shots créme de cacau
1/2 shot vodka
2-1/2 shots half-and-half

Mix all ingredients in a shaker with ice and shake well. Pour into a chilled martini glass.

Sprinkle grated Godiva chocolate on top.